# Eastern Spirituality and Western Psychology

# Eastern Spirituality and Western Psychology

## Revering the Difference

*Meera Sharma,* M.A.
*with Joseph F. Ryan,* PhD

TransPersonal Press
(*a Kaminn Media imprint*)
272 Bath Street
Glasgow G2 4JR
Scotland
transpersonalpress.com



A CIP record for this title is available from the British Library.

ISBN 978-1-912698-06-6 (print)
ISBN 978-1-912698-07-3 (ebook)

Cover photograph: the Tiger Cave at Saluvankuppam, near Mahabalipuram, Tamil Nadu, India. © 2008 Meera Sherma

Edited by Nicky Leach
Cover and text design and layout by Thierry Bogliolo
This book was typeset in Calluna.

Printed, bound and distributed by Ingram Spark

# Contents

**Meera's Dedication** — to the Universe, my Family

All differences in this world are of degree, and not of kind, because oneness is the secret of everything.
—Swami Vivekananda (1863–1902)

The words *Vasudhaiva kutumbakam* ("the world is one family") come from the undated *Maha Upanishad*, which belongs to the Sama Veda tradition. This Upanishad mantra emerged from observation and analysis by the Scientists, who were the Seers and Rishis. This Knowledge was revealed to them when their individualistic identity, the sense of "I am a separate person," was totally lost. Therefore, the sense of "me" was not there to claim "ownership" rights. If you are able to see through the falsity of multiplicity, you will see Oneness.

**Joseph's Dedication** — to the Pilgrims

We are the Pilgrims, master; we shall go
Always a little further; it may be
Beyond that last blue mountain barred with snow
Across that angry or that glimmering sea,

White on a throne or guarded in a cave
There lies a prophet who can understand
Why men were born . . . . [1]

—James Elroy Flecker (1884–1915)

[1] from *The Story of Hassan of Baghdad and How He Came to Make the Golden Journey to Samarkand (Act V, Scene II)*

# Abbreviations and Acronyms

| | |
|---|---|
| b. | Born |
| BCE | Before the Christian era |
| CE | Christian era |
| d. | Died |
| n.d. | Not dated |

# Foreword
### *by Tiger Dragon Storm*

Imagine a world filled with a complete understanding among all of its human inhabitants.

A world where measuring a group of people's philosophical ideas, or scientific contribution to the world, didn't have to adhere to a set of arbitrary rules, such as class or race.

A world where people had profound knowledge of an invisible power that runs equally through all life forms, from the birds to the beetles to the man, woman, and child.

A world where this power was known to exist before the world, and will remain after the world has gone.

A world that recognizes this profound, infinite, and intelligent power was no man in the sky, no alien from another dimension, no philosophical idea; just pure existence uncorrupted by subjective ideas.

A world of humans that all possessed the knowledge that this power was, in fact, fundamentally, what they all are, knowing that the core of themselves—no matter their race, colour, or creed—was this one, single, infinite power that could be experienced when they simply chose to see.

Depending on your cultural, societal, and economic upbringing, your early perspective growing up in this world will be biased towards a particular worldview of what reality is, fundamentally. Is reality a bunch of atoms or quarks like your science teacher taught? Is it a projection of the mind as your spiritual guru taught? Is reality just a mystery that will never be solved? Regardless of how we were raised, we all have an opinion on reality, on God, on truth, on the meaning of life.

Many schools of thought from the East, such as Buddhism, Tantra, Advaita Vedānta, and many more, have provided the world with profound knowledge of what reality is, truly—or at least given the world another means to get to truth, as far as one can with our apparently limited minds.

Famous Western philosophers and spiritual teachers renowned the world over, such as Mooji, Ram Dass, Eckhart Tolle, and Alan Watts, are perfect examples of studying and/or being inspired by the schools of thought previously mentioned.

But who is to say that they, or anybody in the Western spiritual world, is correctly teaching the profound knowledge the East gave us? Or rather, translating and interpreting the teachings in Western languages without losing any of the original meaning or essence?

This is especially true if one is not fluent in Sanskrit, Chinese dialects, or any Eastern language with ties to the ancient spiritual texts, such as the Vedas or the *Tao Te Ching*. Or is truth simply universal, which would mean that there is no correct way to interpret it?

This book, *Eastern Spirituality and Western Psychology: Revering the Difference*, seeks to act as a bridge in understanding the differences between the Western and Eastern understanding of spirituality.

The hypothetical world I mentioned earlier, a world where fundamentally all the people were the same thing, is kind of how it is in our world here on Earth. Instead of calling it a "power," let us call it something we can all agree on, regardless of our beliefs: life energy. We can't have life without the energy to run it! Life energy runs through us all, permeating all we see.

So how is it that this one life energy has a plethora of perspectives worldwide, from culture to culture, on what it actually is? Well, one word sums it up: mind.

It is our minds (as wonderful as they are) that hold our personal perspectives, which creates dissonance in perceiving reality in its purest form. It is our minds, conditioned by particular languages, which automatically limit other minds from understanding each other completely.

This book, a wonderful collaboration between Meera Sharma and Joseph Ryan, points out in great detail just how nuance in language can completely change the meaning of a word or the understanding of a people's beliefs. This publication, therefore, offers a fresh approach, and provides a thrilling exploration into the differences in spiritual understanding between East and West.

There is a relatively new era of spirituality in the West and truth-seeking that veers outside of the Abrahamic religions. We may call it a resurgence, since the dominance of Christianity, Judaism, and Islam did well from their perspective to demonize anyone not following their religions by referring to them as pagans in a less than favourable way. It is important to respect the origins of different cultures' philosophies, if we in the West choose to use them to benefit us in any way.

To be very blunt for a moment, many people have died protecting their ways of life from invaders, so I believe that the least we can do is to respect and learn about other cultures, and (with respect to this book) Eastern cultures and spirituality, properly.

Speaking from the Western perspective but inspired by an Eastern understanding of reality, I see clearly that there are many assumptions we make in the West, either out of ignorance (in the strictest terms meaning "lack of knowledge") or arrogance. For example, Buddhism being referred to as Hinduism, which simply is not correct, as *Eastern Spirituality and Western Psychology: Revering the Difference* explains well.

Interesting differences between how the West approaches religion and how the East approaches it are also covered. Westerners view religion as submitting to an almighty entity as a separate being from themselves; whereas, many Eastern religions are really just a way of life, in which people submit themselves to achieving self-realization, overcoming the ego, overcoming karma, and experiencing oneness with existence, knowing that it is not something unattainable but worth seeking, no matter how many lifetimes it takes.

The first step towards understanding new information is to be open to receiving it. This book doesn't demonize any culture's beliefs; it simply seeks to set the record straight on how the true meaning of Eastern philosophies has sometimes been lost in translation, which should be an interesting notion for you, if you are a truth seeker!

I will use meditation as an example, a topic covered in this book. One of the reasons it is tricky to explain what meditation or Zen is to people in the Western world is due to our lack of practice in simply being still; furthermore, being still and not identifying with any thoughts or sensations that arise within consciousness.

Zen is not a doing, meditation is not a doing; they are a ceasing, a non-doing, which, ironically, is one of the hardest things to do. This is why, no matter where you come from in the world, it must be practised. The difference between the East and West is that Eastern spiritual practices have been embedded in their society for thousands of years, so I guess we could say that they have a good head start! Many more comparisons and well-researched knowledge will be unveiled to you with each turning of a page.

I'd like to finish by, firstly, congratulating Joseph and Meera for their hard work in getting this truly insightful book out into the world and for having me be a part of it.

Secondly, I'd like to quote Meera, who says in the book: "We are all starved of one and the same thing, 'love,' where all differences dissolve."

Whether we call it life energy, power, pure consciousness, or love, we all seek a united world, which begins by understanding we are that power, the love we seek.

Thank you.

—Tiger Dragon Storm

# Preface

When making a relatively short investigation and comparison between Eastern and Western approaches to psychology and spirituality, there are bound to be some generalizations and simplifications. Despite this necessarily broad-brush approach, it is not our intention to stereotype people or cultures; rather, our hope is that this work will draw attention to the unity that lies beneath the apparent differences: we are all one family.

As far as possible, sexist language has been removed: for example, "humankind" instead of "mankind," and so forth. It becomes clumsy to continually write "her or his," so the gender-neutral "their" will be used.

Academia encourages the use of "white literature"; that is, drawing on the most reputable sources of information possible. As a trained historian, Joseph tries to obtain primary source material whenever he can, rather than rely on secondary sources that may contain inaccuracies or misrepresentations; nevertheless, there is much unpublished work and an ever-increasing range of open-source information, especially through the internet, that is worth examining. Much of this material falls into the "grey literature" category.

Ideally, all work cited would be peer-reviewed published texts, but to ignore grey literature entirely would be to lose a vast sea of data. To employ it blindly, however, would be to risk erroneousness or falsehood. Readers, therefore, are encouraged to use their powers of discrimination to separate the wheat from the chaff, the gold from the dross.

If any information is inaccurate or not correctly acknowledged, the authors would be pleased to hear from you. Similarly, any other errors or suggestions can be reported to: msharma669@aol.com or joseph_ryan@btinternet.com. In addition, many books are now read on various mobile devices, which may not provide page numbers from the original text. Nevertheless, as much reference information as possible is given to aid readers, who can also resort to the search function on their digital platform to find specific words or phrases.

# Glossary

This glossary explains a few topics ("Hinduism," "Indology," "Philosophy," "Religious and Spiritual," "Sanskrit," "Translations of Sanskrit words," "Vedas," and "Swami Vivekananda"), in order to build some understanding before going into deep explorational work.

## Hinduism

With respect to Eastern spirituality, the main focus of this book is on "Vedic knowledge." This alone is a vast subject. As such, to consider Buddhism, Jainism, Shintoism, Sikhism, and so forth is beyond the scope of this volume. For the same reason, Christianity is taken as an example of Western spirituality, while Islam and Judaism are not specifically covered. The word "religion" may be mentioned for the purpose of comparison, but these pages are not an examination of any specific religion. Furthermore, the subject of mythology cannot be explored, as this also would require a further publication.

The term "Indian" is subject to clarification and should not be used interchangeably with the word "Hindu," which is closely related etymologically. "Hindu" is misleading because it carries with it the connotation of religion. "Indian" and "Hindu" were never used in India to refer to nationality, culture, philosophy, or religion.

The Indian subcontinent is still called Bharatvarsh (Vedic Foundation 2006) after the name of an ancient king, Bharat, whose name means "lover of knowledge," or in the case of Bharatvarsh, "the land that loves knowledge." *Bha* in Sanskrit means "glory" and "bliss," and the word *rāt* means "being immersed," hence *bharat* means the one who is constantly immersed in the glory of bliss.

In ancient days, it is said, Vedic people lived a cosmic life, which was blissful indeed. When Alexander the Great (356–323 BCE), King of Macedon, invaded the subcontinent in 326 BCE, he crossed the River Sindhu and renamed it the Indus, since it was easier to pronounce in old Persian. Subsequently, the land to the east of the river was called India.

Later, Moslem invaders called the Sindhu River the Hindu River, since in their language, Parsee, the Sanskrit sound "s" converts to "h." Thus, the land east of that river became known as Hindustan. During British rule in India (1757–1947), politicians used the terms "Hindu" and "Hinduism" to differentiate the Hindus from the Moslems ("Moslem" was the common name employed until the first half of the 20th century, but today's usage is "Muslim").

Unfortunately, the misconceptions surrounding the term "Hinduism" makes it virtually a useless word. In India, no religion called Hinduism ever existed. Even today, well-informed spiritual and religious leaders do not use this term. Instead, they call themselves Sanatan Dharmi, which means the followers of "eternal law." During Vedic times, the Indian subcontinent was also known as Āryāvarta, which means "where the Aryan race resides."

Hinduism is not a religion. In fact, all that has emerged from ancient Vedic scripture is non-religious and purely spiritual in nature, and belongs to the entire universe. *Vasudhaiva kutumbakam* is "the voice of the Vedas," meaning the entire world is but one family (*Maha Upanishad*, n.d.). The *Maha Upanishad* belongs to the Sama Veda tradition. The complete meaning of the mantra is: "The distinction 'This person is mine, and this one is not' is made only by the narrow-minded (i.e. the ignorant who are in duality). For those of noble conduct (i.e. who know the Supreme Truth) the whole world is one family (one Unit)" (Vasudaikakutumbam 2015).

This is the pivot of Indian culture: a secure base created by collectivism, enabling people to live life more fully. *Vasudhaiva kutumbakam* is so valuable that it is engraved in the entrance hall of the Parliament of India.

## *Indology*

This is the study of Indian history, languages, literature, and religions by the West.

## *Philosophy*

In the West, philosophy has been divorced from religion, but in the East, it is inseparable. The word for philosophy in Sanskrit is *darśana*, which, according to Chengiah Ragaven's 1999 thesis "The Philosophy of God Consciousness in the Life of Ramakrishna Paramahamsa," means "direct vision." Ragaven says that: "This word highlights a major difference between modern Western philosophy, which predominantly relies on intellectual pursuit and Indian philosophy, which relies on the direct vision of truths and pure *Buddhi* (pure reasoning)."

Another difference is that Indian philosophy is much more comprehensive. Western philosophies and sciences tend to compartmentalize the various aspects of life into distinctly separate disciplines. Only the Aristotelian and medieval Catholic philosophies were able to approach the idea and scope of integration found in Indian philosophy. The major Indian schools integrate into a single framework aesthetics, axiology, epistemology, ethics, logic, metaphysics, physiology, psychology, and sociology. To Indian thinkers, these disciplines are so interrelated that they cannot be served otherwise without losing their vitality.

By "Indian thinkers," what is meant is ancient scientists known as rishis, munis, yogis, and sages who are supposed to be the sources of Vedic knowledge. These beings were considered to be highly evolved and beyond form or need of any significance. This is the very reason the Vedas were not written down for many thousands of years and no one knows who wrote them.

There are even disputes around the author of the *Yoga Sutras of Patanjali*, which were compiled much later than the Vedas and are said to be prehistoric. The translators' foreword reads: "What Patanjali did was to restate yoga philosophy and practice for the man of his own period. But what *was* his period? And who was

Patanjali? Hardly anything is known about him" (Prabhavananda and Isherwood 1953). Indeed, the translators state that there may have been more than one Patanjali: one, the writer of the sutras; the other, a grammarian. The date of the writings, however, may be anywhere between the 4th century BCE and the 4th century CE, a span of 800 years.

Esoteric tradition suggests that it is not recommended to have your name associated with spiritual texts, since it is supposed to reinforce your personal ego. The writings were meant to be unconditional and an anonymous gift to humanity. There is, however, a modern theory about it. Ben-Ami Scharfstein (1919–2019), who was a professor emeritus of Philosophy at Tel Aviv University, Israel, while comparing east-west philosophy, under the chapter of scripture, revelation, and reason, says:

> It holds that the authority of the scriptures is absolute just because they were not composed. The reason given is simple if, to us, surprising: having an author would make the scriptures fallible, while conversely, not having an external source or author would make them infallible . . . . where there is no consequence, there is no cause (Scharfstein 1978).

Accordingly, one can say that Indian philosophy includes theory as well as practice. Indian philosophy addresses all of the natural and spiritual needs of humankind, from the science of medicine to the knowledge of supreme consciousness. It may be considered that although Indian philosophy is not devoid of religion, it is beyond the grasp of religion and, hence, is universal.

The theories and procedures described in the systems of Indian philosophy are not limited to any particular group, culture, or era; rather, they address the universe and ongoing concerns of humanity and are meant for all people. India has always held a holistic approach towards life, which is seen as being composed of two inseparable aspects: life related to the outer world and life related to the inner world, guided by philosophy. No wall stands between philosophy and religion, because both are inextricably interwoven.

This comprehensive approach, including both *dershna* (philosophy) and *sanātana dharma* (eternal law), does not exist in the West. It is, therefore, frequently misunderstood by occidental readers.

These Indian systems appear to be alien to Western minds. Likewise, the Indian mind has a problem understanding the circumscribed notions of philosophy and religion in the West. In Indian culture, the liberty to think freely and to search for the truth personally, independently and experientially, is traditional. As Pandit Tigunait states in *Seven Systems of Indian Philosophy* (Tigunait 1983), "Westerners live freely and think in structured ways, while Easterners think freely and live in structured ways." The West focuses on external nature, indulging in material comforts and technology, while the East is proficient in dealing with inner nature, as its rich tradition of spiritual achievement proclaims.

In the West, there is an overreliance on the medical doctor (as scientist) to deliver a cure with, as described by Caleb Carr in his historical crime novel *The Alienist*, people "running ever faster and in ever greater numbers toward those potions, powders, priests, and philosophies" that promise to eradicate the "fears and nightmares" that encompass their lives (Carr 2018). In the East, however, people try to retain independent health through an ayurvedic diet, traditional medicine, and yoga, coupled with Vedic guidance towards a satisfactory life.

Although India is rich in traditions, only direct experience is thought to bring the answers to the questions of life. As the Upanishads say, "Follow that advice of mine which is good and helpful for your progress, and neglect even my own advice which is not" (Tigunait 1983). It is important, therefore, to resolve these misunderstandings in order to comprehend the concepts and sciences involved. Indian philosophy refers to these concepts and sciences, which are the result of the personal experiences of great sages. The teachings of such sages are universal and meant for the benefit of all humanity. They guide humankind to attain contentment and wisdom here and now. Indian philosophy is a way of life, not a religion. It extends beyond the limits of the senses and the rational mind, and provides methods for attaining experiences of transcendent reality.

## Religious and Spiritual

One of the dictionary meanings for the word "spirituality" is related to its contemporary religious meaning; i.e., it is firmly dualistic, suggesting conditions of being spiritual or having regard for things of the spirit, especially as opposed to material interests (Collins Online English Dictionary 2020).

In *Spirituality: A Brief History* (Sheldrake 2013), Philip Sheldrake details the distinction between religion and spirituality as the latter being based on one's own direct experience, beyond dogma and belief system. The "spiritual" person is not someone who rejects material reality, but rather somebody who trusts the eternal light (consciousness) within and knows through this light that they are capable of dissolving darkness (unconscious/shadow) and accepts this in every life form, which is beyond the structure and dualistic boundaries of religion. Religious life, however, appears to be limited to what is recognized institutionally within a particular culture.

## Sanskrit

The language in which Vedic scriptures is written is known as Sanskrit. It originates from the root word *sanskriti*, which means "culture" or "a process of refinement." Hence, Sanskrit means "that which is totally refined."

It is an ancient language, like Hebrew and Latin. Being the language of the Vedas, it is prehistoric. It has a logical mathematical structure. Every word is divisible into component parts, most of which can be traced to one of about 800 roots. These are monosyllabic sounds representing general qualities of action; moreover, they are said to constitute, as well as represent, the basic energies of the universe.

One root can have many meanings. The language reflects a holistic view of actors and actions as part of a greater whole and a manifestation of a play of polarities. Some abstract nouns contain the meaning of their root, as well as its opposite. For example, according to *The Upanishads* (Shearer and Russell 1978), the concept of unity (*advaita*, or "not two"), unboundedness (*aditi*) and immortality (*amrita*) embrace respectively ideas of duality (*dvaita*), the bounded (*diti*), and death (*mrtyu*). This process is also known as *sandhi vicched*, which means "disjoining."

Understanding the meaning of sentences depends upon knowledge of the meanings of the words. Almost all the major languages of India have come out of Sanskrit. India has two languages (Hindi and English) for official daily work, 22 "scheduled languages" (Wikipedia: Languages with Official Status in India 2019), and 191 languages classified as vulnerable or endangered (Wikipedia: List of Endangered Languages in India 2019). In fact, Sanskrit literature is flexible, polished, expressive, and direct.

## Translations of Sanskrit Words

Some words from the Sanskrit language (such as *akash*) are translated by Meera. Words, however, were checked for accurate translation in *A Sanskrit-English Dictionary: Etymologically and Philologically Arranged with Special Reference to Cognate Indo-European Languages* (Monier-Williams 2011). With other examples of Sanskrit words, a translation can be found in *Śiva Sūtras: The Yoga of Supreme Identity* (Singh 1979), *The Yoga Aphorisms of Patanjali* (Prabhavananda and Isherwood 1953), and *Self-Knowledge* (Śankarācārya 1947). Most of the Indian philosophy books discuss in depth the meaning of Sanskrit words. The challenge was to find a matching or similar word in the English language.

It should be noted that there are no capital letters in Sanskrit. When a Sanskrit word is rendered into English, therefore, the choice of upper or lower case is made by the translator; for example, in capital letters for emphasis or to make it stand it. So, for example, the word *atma* is often written as *Atma*. In addition, some Western translators add the letter "n" to the word, resulting in *Atman*. Similarly, for example, sometimes the letter "a" is added by translators in the word "yoga," although in Sanskrit there is only *yog*. Similarly, the word Vedanta is actually *Vedant* in Sanskrit. These are just some of the many difficulties in translating Sanskrit into other languages.

## *Vedas*

In Indian philosophy and culture, the Vedas are of paramount importance. They were transmitted verbally and constitute the most ancient scriptures known to humankind. Although according to some Western estimations they were compiled around 4000 BCE, there is no proof of that, and Hindus believe them to be prehistoric.

The Vedas were finally written down in the Sanskrit language. Vedic Sanskrit is more ancient than classical Sanskrit. It was known as *Devavani* (*Brahamvani*), meaning "the language of the divine beings." Yāska, who lived in the 4th century BCE, interpreted Vedic Sanskrit words in the *Nirukta* (meaning "explained" or "interpreted") long before Pānini, a highly authoritative grammarian who lived around 500 BCE, systemized classical Sanskrit grammar (Krishnan 2019).

The word *veda* means "knowledge" or "wisdom," with *anta* meaning "end." Hence, the meaning of *Vedānta* is "the end or culmination of the Vedas." The Vedas are the written record of the direct experience of the great sages who realized the truth within. They discovered various methods of meditation to attain higher levels of consciousness. Prose or poetry cannot describe their meaning directly. One needs to know the meta-language or *paribhasa* ("definition") in order to understand them.

Since the teachings of the Vedas and Upanishads address the fundamental questions and problems of human life, they transcend the limitations of culture, place, and time. Students and teachers have always made great efforts to preserve the traditional knowledge.

Vedic teachings have passed continuously from generation to generation as a precious inheritance. In addition, the Sanskrit language has provided the necessary stability and precision for transmitting this knowledge. This is the reason Indian philosophy has maintained its Vedic heritage intact.

The basic Vedic texts are the Rig Veda, Yajur Veda, Sama Veda, and Atharva Veda (Internet Sacred Text Archive 2010). The Rig Veda is a collection of hymns about numerous gods and goddesses, and forces of nature are invoked and glorified through them.

Indian philosophy flows from the profound origin of this Veda. The Yajur Veda focuses on mantras that were used in the performance of healing and medicinal rituals. The Sama Veda discusses the seven notes of music. Sound and its profound impact on the human mind are thoroughly researched within this Veda. The Atharva Veda contains mantras with great supernatural power and is for material gain.

Vedic literature is further divided into four chronological states: Samhita, Brahmana, Aramyaka, and Upanishad (meaning "sitting near devotedly" or "secret teaching") or *Vedānta* (meaning "the end of knowledge"). Each successive stage of Vedic literature represents a development and deepening of both theory and practice.

## Swami Vivekananda

Swami Vivekananda (1863–1902) has always been a major source of inspiration to Meera. He defined life as, "the tendency of the unfolding and development of a being under circumstances tending to press it down" (Rolland 1953). His motto was tolerance and religious universalism. His real name was Narendranath Datta. The name Vivekananda was given by the Maharaja of Khetri, who was inspired by an allusion to the "power of discrimination" possessed by the Swami. He was the founder of Raja Yoga and believed that *Vedānta* should be lived in everyday life. Vivekananda believed his life task was to unite East and West by bringing Western materialism to the East and taking Eastern spiritual treasures to the West. For this reason, he is referred to occasionally in the course of this book.

Vivekananda was born in Calcutta (officially renamed Kolkata in January 2001). He came into contact with Sri Ramakrishna Paramahansa (1836–1886), the "Saint of Dakshineswar," and was transformed by his gentle touch into a great monk and preacher who carried the message of ancient India to the Western world.

Swami Vivekananda's teachings have deeply influenced many people in the United States of America. In many instances, he altered religious conceptions in the direction of an increased appreciation of Hindu ideals. At the Parliament of Religions in 1893, he presented the principles of the Aryan way of life (Belur Math 2019). In 1894, he was the founder of the Vedanta Society of New York (Vedanta Society of New York 2018).

Swami Vivekananda was the first to demand emphatically that even religious beliefs should be subjected to the touchstone of reason and, if found wanting, rejected outright. Speaking on cosmology, he said that the final truth should be in harmony with experience, both within the external world (of science) and the internal world (of spirit). The similarity between the ideas of modern science and *Vedānta* was first anticipated by Swami Vivekananda more than a century ago. This similarity has been confirmed by several scientists, from the physicist Erwin Shrödinger (1887–1961) to physicist, systems theorist, and deep ecologist Fritjof Capra (b. 1939) and is well established now.

Since this book seeks to explore the Vedantic depths of the meanings of words, Vivekananda's approach has been chosen. Although Swami Paramahansa Yogananda (1893–1952) is more popular in the West for his efforts in bringing the East and the West closer, there is a great deal of difference in the way they approached the subject of spirituality.

Vivekananda was a highly intelligent and ambitious person. He knew that the only way for Eastern spirituality to make its way in the West was through the Upanishads (*Vedānta*). His book *From Colombo to Almora* (Vivekananda 1897) reveals much about his work in this field. Rather than trying to bring a new religion to the West, he was promoting universal spirituality in order to bring the light of consciousness to the West. Yogananda's work, however, is quite different. He did not shock the audience, but tried to make his point in a way that the West would find more acceptable and less threatening.

# Introduction

> The truth is right here where you are before you read a
> word of any book. And yet sometimes a decent book can
> be a support for your own real efforts.
> —Brad Warner, *Letters to a Dead Friend About Zen*

After almost two decades, this book emerged from a re-examination and expansion of the concepts and ideas first written by Meera for her 2002 MA thesis in Psychotherapy and Counselling ("The Bridge: Linking the Gap Between Eastern and Western Psychology, Spirituality, Language and Culture") at Regent's School, London.

We look at a particular aspect of human nature known as "difference"—the difference that separates us from each other due to the divisions and boundaries created by cultural, linguistic, and religious gaps. We explore the areas of difference between East and West, and the possibility of "bridging" these gaps. We already understand, for example, that a gap can arise between a therapist and a client when differences of culture, language, philosophy, and religion are not acknowledged and honoured.

This area of study is closely linked to transpersonal psychology, as it can be argued that transpersonal psychology is a product of an East and West merger on a psychological level. Pioneering work began with Carl Gustav Jung (1875–1961) and Aldous Huxley (1894–1963); however, the origin of the term "transpersonal" is largely associated with the human potential movement of the United States in the 1960s, the founding of the *Journal of Transpersonal Psychology* in 1969 by Abraham Maslow (1908–1970) and Anthony Sutich (1907–1976), and the work of Stanislav Grof (b. 1931) and others (Guest 1989; Freeman 2006). The atmosphere of the time was of electric excitement. The introduction of biofeedback, meditation, psychedelics, and yoga brought heights and depths of consciousness to the field of psychology that had never before been dreamt of by Western science.

After more than half a century of infancy and adolescence, transpersonal psychology is arguably now approaching the age of maturity. Fire has turned into flame, but still needs the strength of maturity to dissolve into light (consciousness). An extraordinary potential for growth lies ahead, if only future challenges are met with integrity and rigour. Western psychology has largely overlooked the importance of some very subtle areas of human growth, such as culture, language, and spirituality. By obtaining a deeper understanding of eastern spiritual texts, it is possible to find the source of light and then, perhaps, bridging the gap between East and West will not appear to be so difficult.

In essence, depth psychology is spirituality (and vice versa); thus, whenever spiritual material is used in a loose sense, or superficially, it loses its depth, the source of light is not found, and people remain in the dark. Some spiritual distortions in the field of transpersonal psychology are shown, especially with reference to the work of current writers, such as A. H. Almaas (b. 1944) and Ken Wilber (b. 1949), because their work has gained considerable attention.

We describe some difficult and also remarkable ways in which language has mattered to psychology and spirituality in comparative studies. We examine the role of culture in changing the meaning of words, and its spiritual expression in language, in order to find a place to bridge the East–West gap. We also consider the similarities between East and West, as to bridge the gap, it is essential to understand both the differences and the similarities.

This book is a very small effort towards unfolding the vision of universal unity, a massive task. As such, we shine a light upon only a few areas of difference in the hope that it will then be possible to help pick the right threads in weaving the tapestry of universal unity. It is not about right and wrong. It is about dissolving the differences by acknowledging them, and accepting them as the human attempt towards growth and development, which is the prime task of psychotherapy.

This book is all about the "bridge." It attempts to build bridges across perceived cultural, language, and psycho-spiritual gaps. The East and West are like two fertile lands separated by a river or confluence of various differences. The best way to achieve connection is to build bridges. While bridges do not eliminate divisions, they make it easier for people on both sides to communicate with, and learn from, each other. They make it possible for explorers from one side to reach the other side and further extend their exploratory work. "Bridging" in this context does not only mean to look for similarities on both sides, but most importantly to recognize differences, especially fundamental differences.

In conclusion, seeing similarities can bring people closer but seeing differences enhances our mutual understanding and tolerance. When crossing the bridge, a mindful person will want to find out both how and why some things are similar and others are not. Either way, it is possible to deepen understanding of one's own culture and values, as well as the cultures and values of others.

This book does not attempt to achieve the impossibility of bringing the East and West together, nor wish for Westerners to become Easterners in their minds and outward behaviour, or vice versa. The idea is for the West to join hands with the East in the noble contest for the promotion of the highest ideas, which are the common heritage of the whole world. The evolution of humankind is the evolution of the creative personality. East and West are still conducting experiments on the right ways of living. It seems that primitive ideas of extremism are not going to help humanity to attain the highest step of civilization, for which all are striving. Inner strength, cheerfulness, and selfless service are basic principles of life.

Regardless of whether one lives in the West or the East, people are human beings first, and a real human being is a member of the cosmos (Sharma and Ryan 2017). Geographical boundaries have no power to divide humanity. In order to create a bridge, therefore, it is important to investigate and go to the source of any so-called perceived differences and discover a harmonious place to bridge the gap between East and West.

This idea of bridging the gap between Eastern and Western differences was conceived long before Meera thought of becoming a therapist. She always struggled to express her emotions in English, which is only one of her languages. It seems that the depth and current of her feelings do not always match the vocabulary available in English and, therefore, unpleasant compromises have to be made. It feels like drinking champagne from a plastic cup. Meera's own cultural conditioning, however, helps her to accept life as it is. Life happens; it cannot be planned. There is a reason for things to be the way they are. As such, it is necessary to learn to trust the process of life and accept ignorance about any unexplored potentials.

About her personal background and history, Meera says:

> I come from an extended family in India. My parents were quite traditional and lived a very spiritual life. I guess my father had a sense of superiority for being a Brahmin by caste. For a long time, I also enjoyed this sense of superiority for belonging to a high caste, until the time when I began to question, "Who am I?" I learnt much about old-world scriptures from my father and my elder brother. I still miss that atmosphere of spiritual discussions in our family gatherings and the energy of that passion which, even today, I feel in my body. Now, in hindsight, I can see these discussions masked many prejudices and, perhaps unconsciously, seeded a desire within me to unmask these prejudices. That was the background for this present investigation. Even as a young girl, I had a strong fascination with the other world. I had so many questions about everything around me and often used to get into trouble with my parents, who felt anxious about my deep interest in exploring the unconscious. In school, Sanskrit was my favourite subject. I loved the depths of Sanskrit poetry, such as the lyric poem "Meghadūta" by Kālidāsa [c. 4th–5th century CE]. At the same time, I equally enjoyed the poetry of William Wordsworth [1770–1850] and the sonnets of William Shakespeare [1564–1616]. I used

to "steal" my father's books to read about "esoteric stuff," as my father did not think that I was at the right age to read such books. After he died, I brought some of his books (which are very rare) here to England with me, including some old Indian volumes that did not even have any details printed on them as required by modern bibliographic standards.

Meera came to England in 1967, and the seed of this book started to sprout. Her father had once instructed her that a person must learn to greet others properly. For example, the posture while making the common Indian greeting *Namaste* has a deep spiritual significance. It means that "I bow my head (the highest part of my body) to greet your soul." At that time, this explanation seemed satisfactory, but it was just the beginning. As Meera learnt more about chakra yoga, she discovered that the five fingers of each hand are connected to our five lower chakra energies. After the fifth, or "throat," chakra (*vishuddha*), all the other chakras come together at the sixth, or "third eye," chakra (*ajna*). This is the "uniting centre" of all human potential. After this, the seventh, "crown" or "thousand-petaled," chakra (*sahasrara*) is the gateway to our divine nature. (For more on the chakra system, see Anodea Judith's 2004 book *Eastern Body, Western Mind: Psychology and the Chakra System as a Path to the Self*.) So when people place both hands together, they are bringing together their total energies and meeting another person at the "essence level," as a whole.

As an example of so-called differences between the East and West, Easterners appear to greet others on the essence level and maintain an attitude of passivity and contemplation, whereas Westerners greet others on a personality level and maintain an attitude of activity (shaking hands) and goodwill. This is quite an interesting insight into an important difference between the East and West. In Western custom, people greet each other by shaking with their right hands, thereby utilizing the left side of the brain, which is concerned with logic and logical tasks; so it might be argued that they exchange those logical energies, or at least it symbolically suggests that they are most concerned with such energies. It is also known as "putting your weapons down" and meeting another person in love and peace. It seems that it is conveying a very important message, but on an unconscious level of communication.

Culture, language, and spirituality, therefore, affect the meaning and understanding conveyed through various methods of communication. Certainly, Joseph is aware that his Western upbringing affects perception and understanding. He remarks:

> Born an Englishman, I was schooled in a Judeo-Christian culture that relies on logical, scientific thought that expresses itself in technological advances and materialism. In particular, with a father born in the south of Ireland, it was almost inevitable that I should be baptized and raised as a Roman Catholic. Held as the "one true church," the Catholic Church simply regarded proponents of other religions, with their various gods, as benighted heathens. I neither mixed with people of other faiths nor studied their beliefs. This was a narrow curriculum, and my horizons only slowly widened due to voracious and disparate reading, and perhaps because my mother was born and lived in India (Uttar Pradesh) until her 20s and conveyed to me a more elastic worldview and religious tolerance. Her tales coloured my childhood and, together with a karmic inheritance hot-wired into my genes, my dreams were peopled with goddesses from the subcontinent that were shunned in my waking life. When I was about seven years old, I was wise enough to know that praying to Jesus Christ for toys or other tat was a dead end. After much consideration, I knelt and humbly asked God for the gift of wisdom. When Odin, god of the Norsemen, gained wisdom, it was only after he had been crucified on the Tree of Life, Yggdrasil, and had one eye plucked out, to boot. Likewise, what wisdom I developed came at a price and during the course of a long journey.
>
> Like many Westerners, I dabbled in many spiritual practices hoping to find enlightenment. First came the

martial arts: karate, kendo, t'ai chi chuan, and ninjutsu. I also studied then practised counselling, focusing on a transpersonal approach. As such, I examined Western alchemy, yoga, and so on. My most consistent spiritual practice has been *Seon* (Zen) Buddhism with the Korean Jogye Order. This has allowed me to go deeper, rather than drift across many paths, which is perhaps a Western tendency—a hope that one more workshop, course, or speaker, gee-jaw, or honeyed promise will bring insight, delivered speedily and at a reasonable cost and, of course, without inconvenience or effort. Any serious spiritual endeavour, therefore, is handicapped by a cultural norm that expects that everything has a monetary value and is available in the marketplace for the one prepared to pay. Frustration and eventual disappointment are then inescapable. My journey continues to this day, but now I largely look inside—not to the exterior world—for guidance and realization.

From reading books by Stanislav Grof and Ken Wilber, it was clear that their interpretation of Eastern esoteric texts was different from Meera's understanding. It seemed obvious that one of the reasons for this might be that neither Grof nor Wilber lived in the land of the language long enough to assimilate the culture that was being voiced through the words of that language, thus resulting in a distortion of the meaning of the old texts.

Meera recounts that when she read *Grace and Grit* (Wilber 1991), in which Wilber wrote about his own anguish but being supported by his spirituality while his wife was dying of cancer, the depth of his experience felt so real that she says that it, "moved every cell in my body. There was a flow (a holistic sensation associated with the act of total involvement) and lucidity voicing through his words which deeply touched me." But when Wilber talks about Eastern traditions and spirituality, his words seem to be just words; somehow, the connection with the voice of holistic experience appears to be missing. Such perceived distortions from Western interpretations led her to further explore the differences in areas such as culture, language, psychology, and spirituality, which will be explored subsequently.

It seems that human psychology is not a unitary process. It cannot, therefore, possibly offer a holistic way of life. It may need different things and take different courses under different circumstances and at different times. Meera states that, "My mind started searching for these differences at every possible opportunity."

In particular, she was inspired by *Comparative Philosophy: Western, Indian, and Chinese Philosophies Compared* (Bahm 1977). Archie J. Bahm (1907–1996) observes that while Hindus encourage passivity and Europeans encourage activity, the need for both is accepted by the Chinese, stating, "Every being (*tao*) consists of both *yang* and *yin* . . . . Being and doing are equally important, equally natural, equally good."

In the West, the work of A. H. Almaas, Ken Wilber, and John Welwood (1943–2019) in the field of transpersonal psychology has gained a great deal of attention. When the work of Almaas is compared to the style and approach of Wilber, it is interesting to notice the difference in their approach to transpersonal issues.

Almaas was born in Kuwait and moved to the United States at 18 years old. His cultural background allows him to demonstrate both strength and vulnerability in the message he is conveying, and a deep grasp and understanding of the meaning of transpersonal issues.

In an article entitled "The Pearl Beyond Price" in *Yoga Journal*, Almaas's student and psychotherapist Dr. Don Flory writes: "Almaas looks at spiritual awakening as part of a developmental continuum that begins at birth, includes the various stages of ego formation and deformation, and can continue beyond ego to the highest states of mystical consciousness. His teachings blend esoteric spiritual terminology with the technical language of clinical psychology . . . . In the Diamond Approach [Almaas 1998], this classic mystical goal is accomplished using many of the tools and theories of modern Western psychology."

Unlike Wilber, who sees the personal and transpersonal stages as sequential (suggesting that, at a certain point, people finish their psychological work and move on to spiritual issues), Almaas views the personal and transpersonal as entwined all the way to the higher states of consciousness. As Almaas puts it in his interview with Flory: "At the beginning of our psychospiritual quest, we struggle with the current crises in our lives. As we develop spiritually, we must uproot habits and beliefs acquired at earlier and earlier periods in our development."

A comparison between Almaas and Wilber helps to establish the role of culture and language in relating to the understanding of the meaning of an experience. It can be argued that cultural differences may have influenced their thinking, which appeared in translations of their texts.

The possibility of different languages embodying different forms of understanding can be seen as another reason for this variation in their thinking. In *Philosophy East/Philosophy West: A Critical Comparison of Indian, Chinese, Islamic, and European Philosophy* (Scharfstein 1978), Ben-Ami Scharfstein regards words as having "field properties" and categorizes the field into which they are organized as linguistic, conceptual, or semantic. According to Scharfstein, a semantic field is an alliance of words so ordered as to categorize and express a distinct area of experience. Because the words in a field are ordered, the meaning of each is dependent on that of the other. Thus, the difference from a psychological standpoint can be viewed as linear understanding of the Eastern text by Wilber, resulting in distortion of the meaning of the text, whereas a spontaneous unfolding allowed by Almaas expressed the depth of his experience. Wilber seems to be settling for a superficial meaning of the words, whereas Almaas appears to be diving into the depths of their meaning.

Metaphorically speaking, perhaps one could say that an Eastern recipe followed by a Western cook may not produce the same results, because the end product involves the integration of everything that contributed towards the creation of the recipe: the person involved in preparation, their culture, their feelings, their language, their philosophy, their thinking, and even their sense of self. The idea of a recipe seems appropriate here since it is experiential: one has to taste the dish to appreciate it; just reading the recipe leaves one with questions and a sense of incompleteness.

Since language is considered to be metaphoric by nature, it can be argued, therefore, that even metaphorically speaking, it seems important to remember that metaphors are mostly used in a partial sense and that they, too, get culturally interpreted. There is always some aspect in the metaphor that is excluded. The same is also true for difference, as someone truly knows the difference through a "felt sense"; one feels difference at a very much deeper level. Perhaps it is so deep, subtle, and unconscious that most of the time a person is not even aware of its existence. Such subtle differences need to be first acknowledged before they can be worked out on a conscious level of awareness.

Holistic growth unfolds by nature, and the language of Eastern texts, which draw on the experiences of the sages of old (in ancient scripture), requires a mind capable of grappling with the spontaneous nature of the language in order to receive the "essence" of the scriptures. It could be argued that it is hard for Western authors to connect with such spontaneity in the language of the text, while trying to understand it through their linear way of thinking. The same can be said of Eastern authors who manifest their discontent about the West by condemning it for its materialism and not being self-reflective.

Perhaps, for deep transformation to take place, the death of "who you think you are" is important. It requires working with all those things that bring comfort and being willing to let go of that comfort through the realms of different kinds of neurosis, such as despair and crisis.

Perhaps ego structure in the West is different from that of the East. In the West, God is perceived as distant, allowing one to be judged by Him, whereas in the East, one's ego is tied to family and community structure, and people are conscious of a greater social and spiritual totality. In spiritual practice, the basic question is not about the particular structure of the individual or collective ego, which is in the realm of the content of the mind; it actually focuses on the nature of the activity of mind. The work in practice is to harmonize both perspectives. The work of fusion is directed towards dissolving such fears (through practices) that get in the way of people facing their own truth. Ultimately, peace is only acquired by realizing one's own truth.

Although psychological growth is very different from spiritual growth, none of this is to deny that psychology is an integral part of spirituality. They enhance one another and cannot be separated, just as the East and the West are two poles, always co-creating and bringing forth their unique expressions in the form of art and science to unite their diverse natures. It is unfortunate, therefore, that in the West, as Maxwell Maltz says in the preface to his 1960 book *Psycho-Cybernetics*, "Psychology, which began with the study of man's psyche, or soul, almost ended by depriving man of his soul" (Maltz 1960). Psychology, from the Greek, means "study of the soul," but this is the last thing that traditional psychology would consider examining. There is no research grant or funding for the study of the scientifically unmeasurable, such as "soul" or even "love." So, people are offered a truncated, stunted understanding of human beings and their divine potential.

On this matter, Joseph says that:

> Western psychology speaks of body, mind, and emotions, but forgets about soul (even if the term is derived from the Greek word psyche, meaning soul). I obtained a Master's degree in psychology, studying the brain to cellular level, but the mind and the soul proved elusive topics. Western academia believes that science is the valid primary tool to examine our world. In the process, it considers anything that cannot be measured as of little consequence, whether that be love, spirit, or God.

In "Trans-personal & Psychology of the Vedic System: Healing the Split Between Psychology & Spirituality" in the *International Journal of Yoga and Allied Sciences*, Meera Sharma summarizes this point thus: "Psychology is a secular science, while spirituality is a sacred art" (Sharma 2015a).

From a clinical point of view, it is perhaps not possible for a therapist to simply decide to be a transpersonal therapist. In Meera's experience, despite her Eastern spiritual background, she went from being a traditional therapist to being a transpersonal or spiritual therapist over a period of several years, during which time her own worldview, values, and goals for herself all changed. It would not have been possible for her to become a transpersonal therapist simply by hearing someone else was doing it and that it sounded like a glamorous idea.

An awareness of imbalance and recognition of the resulting disharmony are necessary before the depth of spirituality can be integrated in current psychological culture. Psychological growth is very different from spiritual growth. Perhaps one could argue that psychology deals with the effects only, whereas spirituality deals with the cause in order to facilitate holistic transformation.

The focus of Western psychology seems to be on developing a functional ego structure to enable people to cope adequately and effectively with existing culture. This leads to finding meanings instead of making connections and developing understanding. Western psychology does not appear to investigate the depth of one's identification with the ego structure. It appears that traditional psychology is primarily interested in worldly adjustments, happiness, and achievements, whereas a holistic and transpersonal stance appears to be more subjective in nature.

Meera states that:

> At times, I have felt angry about the distortions caused by differences between Western and Eastern values, and about not being understood and accepted by Western culture. I tried to fight it with arguments and in defensive situations. I have also used egoistical expressions of my opinions, which did not help at all in clarifying or developing my understanding of what I wanted to put across. I struggled with my anger until such time when I was able to recognize my own inner disturbance. Somewhere in the depths of my heart, I wanted to break through this "difference" between the East and West, and wanted to embrace the love I sought so much. This realization helped me to overcome my anger, and I became less opinionated. I learnt we are all starved of one and the

> same thing, "love," where all differences dissolve. Again, however, love and fear cannot live together. Unfortunately, the majority of us live in fear most of the time. I suppose it is hard to survive in this world without fear. Right at this very moment I may have several fears, which I may be resisting expressing. An awareness of my "fear" helps me to reduce my anxiety, but not being able to express it still leaves me with feelings of sadness for holding back my "truth."

We might consider that as spiritual beings in a physical world there is only one consciousness and that we are all part of the "Oneness." When it comes to us seeking to express this understanding, unfortunately, it often seems that the literature available is inadequate to the task. Meera requests that the readers understand that the evidence from which she originally learnt this information is not important in itself. She was raised in an Indian spiritual-cultural environment. The information, in most cases, could be completely changed to different information without affecting the outcome. Meera also says:

> In addition, I have made many mistakes as I am just human on that level. Although, it is interesting to know that every time I made a mistake it led me into a deeper understanding of the reality and a higher truth. I will request, therefore, that if you find an error, look deeper. Maybe my culture and language are also getting in my way of making the point I so wish to make. I will be quoting my personal experiences where appropriate. They may sound outrageous by the ordinary world's standards, but it is for you to decide if they are true or not, for if you really listen deeply with your heart, your heart always knows the truth. As the Chandogya Upanishad proclaims, one "sees, hears, reflects, understands, acts, and knows" (Sivananda 2011).

As authors, the means at our disposal for this undertaking are totally inadequate. We tread on dangerous ground, therefore, taking a huge risk by not being adequately equipped to fulfil the intent of this book. There is no clear-cut methodology that can be put forward for research on this subject, because there is no simple way to demonstrate that it is a common reality that people are experiencing disharmony in the present multicultural society, due to being faced with particular challenges of difference. There is very little, if any, awareness about the fear of exposure to these issues of culture, language, and spirituality that are keeping us apart.

This work is based on our own experiences, subjective and objective, and to a large extent on the reading of old texts and modern authors who have tried to make connections to current situations by adopting a spiritual route. Other than this, comparative philosophy is loosely used as a method of bridge-building. Most philosophers tend to philosophize within their same culture and traditions, which seems rather limited. Comparative philosophy across traditions and cultures can broaden horizons. Drawing from different philosophies provides different perspectives and sheds new light on issues in any particular culture. It can help open minds to generate new and creative insights and be more accepting of differences.

In this research, the goal of comparative philosophy is not to prove one view right and the other wrong. It is about comparing doctrines and beliefs in major traditions, which may have survived for thousands of years and proved themselves within their own contexts over time. The emphasis remains upon the processing of ideas and beliefs, their evolutionary development, and their implications for the future. Most importantly, comparative philosophy takes cross-cultural translation seriously and explores what is meant by translation. This method can support our work. The Indian system, furthermore, did not used to study psychology as a separate subject, seeing it instead as an integral part of Indian philosophy. Comparative philosophy, therefore, can help enhance Eastern views.

Although a certain level of criticism is necessary for correction and exploitation of potentials, it is not the purpose of this book. It may appear critical sometimes, but that is only for the purpose of teasing out the differences. Another important point to notice here is that this book is not specifically about spirituality. It only seeks to investigate the spiritual dimensions of some words from old texts. For this reason, it explores (on a very elementary level) the origin and differences of prevailing spirituality in both the East and West, discussing how meanings are misunderstood and mis-interpreted, looking at distortions caused by such imbalances, the perceived outcome of this, and the impact and consequences.

In addition, part of the purpose of this study is to investigate the differences in the meanings of Sanskrit words as used by West-ern writers and the part played by culture, language, and spiritu-ality in changing the meaning of these words.

Due to the unacknowledged part played by these factors, transpersonal psychology (which appears to bring a spiritual di-mension to traditional psychology) is experiencing a transitional crisis. It seems that while integrating Eastern spiritual dimensions into modern psychology, greater emphasis has been placed on psy-chology and very little importance is placed on the awareness of spirituality. Perhaps transpersonal psychology and psychotherapy needs to address the broadest conceptualization possible for human psychological growth. This includes (along with comfort and gratification in one's relationship with self, family, work, and society) recognition of the yearning for meaning, purpose, and transcendence of self-consciousness as part of our nature.

It appears that transpersonal psychology and psychotherapy presuppose the existence of a spiritual dimension in human be-ings, and being a transpersonal therapist presupposes sharing this conviction. Although the field is not limited to any particular sys-tem, religious or spiritual, it appears to recognize just the validity of spiritual systems in general and not the yearning for spiritual unfolding as one of the givens of human growth and development.

Most of the theories discussed in this book are largely based on our own observations, experiences, and insights. While our theories are supported as much as possible by appropriate refer-encing, this has been made difficult by the relative paucity of written work on this subject. In the absence of such support from the literature, therefore, it is a problem to prove a point by relevant evidence.

The main focus is on the differences, particularly when we have felt impressed or challenged by the texts we have read. Resources are drawn from both Eastern and Western texts. In order to understand the actual meaning of a word, it is important to have some basic knowledge and understanding of the culture, history, and philosophy of that language. (To help clarify, a brief account of Indian philosophy may be found in the Glossary.)

In many ways, ancient Eastern spirituality is a current subject of discussion within present-day psychology. Because of the great number of religions and spiritual disciplines to be found in society, this investigation is primarily limited to Christian spiritual traditions and the Vedic (Hindu) way of living. The main concentration is on the differences between the two disciplines and the possibility of bridging this gap.

The hypothesis to be tested in this book is to consider the East and West as two opposing poles. Cynicism in the West, caused by materialism, has led it increasingly to be attracted to Eastern spirituality and simplicity. The scientific-minded and extrovert West appears to be struggling to understand the introvert nature and depth of the Eastern heart.

Opposites procreate new meanings; thus, the possibility of a new language, culture, and identity is emerging. We have discovered that language limits our experience of the "realities" encountered in both mysticism and the new physics, yet our linguistic ways of thinking dominate our life. We do not realize that outside the narrow plane of words there may be vast realms of conscious experience that we are denying ourselves because we have been culturally conditioned to think with words. As the Tibetan Buddhist Tilopa (988–1069 CE) wrote in the *Song of Mahamudra* (Washington 2014): "Though words are spoken to explain the Void, the Void as such can never be expressed. Though we say 'the Mind is a bright light,' it is beyond all words and symbols. Although the Mind is void in essence, all things it embraces and contains." To experience reality beyond our verbal training, we must retreat back to nonverbal realms, but it is not the purpose of this book to cover them here.

Since this book specifically investigates synthesized meanings of Sanskrit words, which are a mixture of culture, language, philosophy, and spirituality, it is important to be able to distinguish between both Eastern and Western views of these aspects.

Chapter 1 investigates the definition and fundamental differences in Eastern and Western spirituality. The chapter explores the differences that function as barriers and raise challenges, and (the challenge having been raised) how they could possibly function as bridges as well. The chapter shows how basic problems in any tradition may not be so in another tradition; understanding this requires a holistic shift across traditions. Chapter 2 explores the role of language and culture in changing meanings of Sanskrit words by reflecting on meanings perceived by the West. Chapter 3 looks at distortions by the Western world, on things such as meditation and yoga, assumptions about religion, traditions, and culture, and further investigates whether the Western world could ever understand ancient Eastern wisdom as it is, without distortions. Chapter 4 focuses on the implications for psychotherapy. Finally, there is a summary of the authors' conclusions in Chapter 5.

Writing this book was a huge challenge and led to anxiety about dealing with our inadequacies and limitations. The idea behind this book, however, is to present a holistic picture of our views and ideas regarding an Eastern mindset, as well as any concerns and conclusions. As passionate transpersonal therapists (with Meera, in particular, a keen student of *Vedānta* psychology), our concerns are not just about transpersonal psychology that, in a crude sense, is misdiagnosing psychological issues by little knowledge of the subject about which it is claiming to be expert, but also the impact that this may have on humanity at large, and how this does not seem to be considered.

# Chapter 1

# Spiritual Development
# in the East and West

East is East, and West is West,
and never the twain shall meet.
—Rudyard Kipling (1865–1936),
*The Ballad of East and West*

This chapter explores differences between Eastern and Western spirituality. Firstly, we briefly examine the development of the philosophic foundations of spirituality in the West and then explore the current position of spirituality. Finally, we consider the definition of spirituality.

Indian philosophy suggests the spiritual nature of the Sanskrit language. Although it is integral, spirituality is the fundamental aspect behind the meaning of Sanskrit words. It is important, therefore, to understand how spirituality has been viewed within both cultures and what part spirituality has played in the development of these cultures, societies, and nations. Finally, we consider the present position of spirituality within both cultures.

It can be argued that the notion of spirituality is not identical in all religions, and all spirituality has sprung from a psychological urge. Starting from an antithesis between the carnal and the spiritual, between the flesh and the spirit, it seems Christian spirituality has travelled a long way.

In the language of Christianity, the urge behind all spirituality may be described as people's love of life, or the product of their unwillingness to submit to the laws of nature and biology. Being aware of the limitations of their existence and powers imposed by nature, humankind appears to have persistently refused to submit to them. In order to evade this, perhaps, people have tried to find a way around it by creating a subjective world in which their existence will be eternal and their aspirations undisrupted. In other words, driven by such arrogance, this could have been humankind's way of revolting against nature.

In *Hinduism: A Religion to Live By* (Chaudhuri 1962), Nirad C. Chaudhuri (1897–1999) writes that man has always resented his limitations, old age, disease, and inevitable death, and has been eagerly engaged in trying to overcome them, especially death. Indeed, it was the sight of an old man, a sick man, and a dead body that propelled Prince Siddhārtha on his spiritual journey to become the Buddha (c. 480–c. 400 BCE). It is the idea of man's own death, which is inescapable, that frightens him most. In order to get rid of this sense of impermanence and insecurity, he created a double of his physical life, by believing that life is an external and indestructible element that enters and leaves the destructible material body. An image of life, therefore, was created around life and death. The idea of resurrection in Christianity has been most powerful, giving hope for eternal life. By observing the function of breath, which ceases at death, the idea of the existence of spirit is seemingly confirmed.

Chaudhuri further writes that this idea of spirit gave birth to the idea of a spirit world, similar to the material world. This idea of a spirit world was imagined to be more powerful and immortal. From this idea of a spirit world originated the word "god" or "gods." Powerful and mysterious forces of nature were also perceived as an extension of the idea of a spirit world. It is hard to prove how all these mental creations took place, but they are closely connected and formed the basis of most elementary forms of spirituality in the West.

Gradually, this idea developed and further evolved to the level of divinity. The highest moral ideals of transcendental Christianity made their God so perfect and absolute that He became unattainable even by them. They could only surrender unto Him in a spirit of humility and devotion. Perhaps this is why it would be relatively rare for Westerners to devote themselves entirely and exclusively to a guru (a Hindu imparter of spiritual knowledge, not to be confused with a teacher, who is primarily an educator). Such devotion would be seen as belonging only to God.

As Chaudhuri notes, the idea of the separateness of two worlds and human limitations established that strength for Christians, who had to be made perfect in their weakness. The power of such intense psychological contact with the transcendental world produced a bodily effect and, thus, from this combination of bodily and mental reaction originated "mysticism," described by Chaudhuri as "the most concentrated form of Christian spirituality." This kind of spirituality was not totally self-contained and partly overlapped with the intellectual and moral field. As a result, Christian faith has been based on reason. Even Pascal approved of the validation of reason when he said, "*Le cœur a ses raisons, que la raison ne connaît point*" ("The heart has its reasons, which reason knows nothing of"). This spirituality had a profound effect on human behaviour by bringing about a catharsis of man's natural impulses. On the other hand, it appears that Hindu religious sentiment never took this line of development and remained true to the original motivation of spirituality, which was to become free from all the restraints imposed on humans by nature through developing understanding and making a connection with nature through one's own experience of it, thus dissolving the fear that imposes restraint between man and nature.

The laws of nature can be very deceiving, too, until and unless one has gone beyond nature. Hindu spirituality, which is a relentless pursuit for truth, proclaims in the Rig Veda (1.164.46) that "*Ekam sat vipra bahudha vadanti,*" meaning that "truth is one but expounded in many ways by the wise" (Menon 2006). In his 1996 book *Primal Spirituality of the Vedas: Its Renewal and Renaissance*, R. Balasubramanian puts this very clearly, stating that within Hinduism one can argue on any subject since it has no hierarchy nor any establishment or governing body. Actually, in Sanskrit there is no word for spirituality, nor was there any reference to the word in the modern Indian language until recently. The notion was introduced through the English language. The word equivalent to spiritual is known as *adhyatmik*, which means "study of the self." Even this translation feels superficial, since these Sanskrit words possess meditational and transpersonal qualities in their very pronunciation beyond the literal meaning. If you think about the word "spiritual," what comes to your mind? What do you feel about it? How deeply it is able to touch your soul, or not even touch your soul nature at all, remains in the category of mind. But when she utters the word *adhyatmik*, it takes Meera to her understanding of Higher consciousness (*Atma*). She feels connected to her Being.

As Meera understands the culture and the language, she feels unsatisfied with this translation. Although the "study of self" sounds like a meaningful description, it does not do justice to the word *adhyatmik*. If we use the Sanskrit method of *sandhi vicched* (disjoining), it will read *adhyan atmik*. Now the word *adhyan* is emerging from the word *dhyāna*, which in English is translated as "meditation," so *adhyan* translated to read "study" is like a body without a soul; it has lost its vitality; it is like orange or banana peel, the remains of fruit. It reminds one of the fruit, but it is not actually what one wanted to eat.

Similarly, attempts by modern philosophers to translate the word *Atma* as the word "Self" does not do justice to this word. "Self" is a psychological term, in a very subtle way relating to the mind. It is also material, only finer, and it is not *Atma*.

It is perhaps very hard to translate *Atma* into English. It is so spiritual that maybe it can only be realized through experience. We can only make a very sad compromise by using this universally accepted word "Self." As Jaideva Singh states in *Śiva Sūtras: The Yoga of Supreme Identity* (Singh 1979): "Atma is the real man. . . . It is the Atma that uses the material mind as its instrument, like eyes are not the real organs of vision." *Atma*, as described in the Vedic texts, is the spiritual essence in all creatures, their real innermost essential Being. It is eternal; it is the essence; it is beyond time and space. *Atma* is that which one is at the deepest level of one's existence.

In the West, *Atma* is considered "a metaphysical and spiritual concept for the Hindus, often discussed in their scriptures with the concept of Brahman" (Wikipedia: Ātman [Hinduism] 2020). Meera's personal understanding of *Atma*, however, is more like: I have a body, but I am not my body; I have a mind, but I am not my mind; I have a soul, but I am not even my soul. From her knowledge of the Vedic texts, that I am *Atma*, waiting to be one (i.e., unite) with *pram-atma* (Ultimate Reality). As I am, I am just a shadow, or dark aspect (macrocosm/microcosm), of the Godhead (*pram-atma*) continuously moving towards the Light of Consciousness to dissolve my shadow and to realize "*Aham Brahmasmi!*" (I am the absolute reality). The final aim, therefore, is to realize one's own True Nature, which is divine and pure; to realize through self-enquiry "*Who am I?*"

This concern for the Self, *adhyatmik*, refers to the relation of the Self to the cosmos, which has a greater meaning than it is possible to discuss here. Chaudhuri states that the vastness and depth of Vedic texts are so immense that if one is not open enough to the verity presented in them, it can lead to a great deal of confusion and misunderstanding. This confusion appears very much present in the translation of old texts by present Western authors.

German-born Oxford University Professor of Comparative Philology Friedrich Max Müller (1823–1900) expressed that "the religion of the Veda knows of no idols" (Stone 2002). Also, as stated in the Jābāla Upanishad, "Yogis should find god within their own selves, and not in images; the latter are meant only as aids to meditation for the ignorant" (Morgan 1987).

Similarly, Islam has a strong tradition of adherence to aniconism, which is the custom, or belief, of avoiding any graphic representation of religious figures or godly beings, although Muslims frequently extend this to representations of human beings or animals (Khan 2012). Representations of the Prophet Muhammed (571–632 CE), of course, have historically provoked outrage; for example, when the French satirical publication *Charlie Hebdo* published a cartoon image of Muhammed on its front cover (Nelson 2015).

Picking up subjects randomly from Hindu scriptures could be confusing since, on the one hand, *Advaita* talks about *Brahma* (infinite) alone and, on the other hand, Hindu mythology is filled with all kind of stories about thousands of gods and goddesses. Hinduism is an exemplar of unity in diversity. It might be argued that the occidental writers who have dealt with Hindu spirituality have never clearly understood this greater meaning, which has been lost in translation.

In *Philosophy East/Philosophy West: A Critical Comparison of Indian, Chinese, Islamic, and European Philosophy*, Ben-Ami Scharfstein remarks about the seriousness of cross-cultural translation and difference: "It is only too easy to lift ideas out of their cultural contexts, to translate the terms in which they are expressed into familiar ones, and to come to plausible but misleading conclusions" (Scharfstein 1978). This is the very point this book attempts to make: that to reduce the risk of further distortions, it is important to be aware of the differences that may be clouding one's perception of another's world.

Philosophy in India has sprung from the spiritual experiences of the ancient sages; it is not the result of mere intellectual speculation. Since it aims at the knowledge of the Transcendental Reality, it is termed in Sanskrit *darśana*, or "vision of truth." One can say that every Indian school of philosophy holds the view that there is a direct realization of Truth. In the ultimate analysis, Hindu spirituality is interwoven with the cosmos. Hindu spirituality and Hindu phenomenal existence are inseparable; they stand together in that respect. Thus, as Mysore Hiriyanna notes in his 1949 book *Essentials of Indian Philosophy*, Hindu spirituality, which is a pursuit of Truth, seems to have a multifaceted meaning.

The most obvious contrast is to be seen between its introvert expression and its extrovert expression. The first is seen in the Way of Knowledge, and the second in the Way of Action. Both are important aspects of Hindu spirituality. The introvert form, which is the creation of the Way of Knowledge, is the one that has given Hindus their current reputation for spirituality. This never broke with the original motivation of Hindu spirituality, which is the desire to overcome the limits of human existence and to be free from all the limitations on human power imposed by nature.

According to Sri Sankarācārya in his 1947 book *Self-Knowledge: An English Translation of Śaṅkarāchārya's Ātmabodha*, Hindus in their quest for immortality and indestructibility through the Way of Knowledge did not create a transcendental world in which human beings could have eternal life. They looked for indestructibility, not only for themselves but also for the entire universe. They hit upon the idea that behind all manifested phenomena (which were subject to change and thus also to destruction), there existed (consubstantial with them and yet inaccessible to the senses) an unmanifested, attribute-less, unchangeable, all pervasive element that was eternal and indestructible. They also formulated the corollary, that phenomena were only particular parts of a general and absolute reality. This idea seemed to have arrived very early in the history of human civilization, yet is similar to that which has been discovered by modern physics in recent times (see Kassel 1922; Capra 1975; Zukav 1979).

As Hiriyanna notes, it is generally agreed within Hindu text that the spirituality of the Way of Knowledge is a quest of power for inner life, which gives one the capacity to rise above the termination of selfhood and the destruction of all things outside the self. In contrast, the spirituality of the Way of Action is orientated towards actions in the form of unobstructed self-assertion. Its object is to acquire the capacity to do things beyond what is within the natural physical and mental powers of humans; for example, the capacity to see into the future, read the minds of others, control physiological processes, even disregard the laws of gravity. In short, they developed the capacity to perform miracles. The spirituality of the Way of Action, therefore, can be regarded as a specialized and highly intensified form of the general religious practices of the Hindus. Karma yoga sought these powers through human effort, special psychological and physical exercises, and, above all, self-mortification.

## Differences

These accounts of Eastern and Western spirituality provide sufficient understanding of the fundamental differences between them. It seems that Western spirituality is very much extroverted in nature and places emphasis on a God who is other than ourselves, while Eastern spirituality is introverted and places emphasis on true human nature. The difference is not fundamental, but it is important. According to Swami Prabhavananda, as stated in *The Yoga Aphorisms of Patanjali* (Prabhavananda and Isherwood 1953), the "value of the Christian approach is that it heightens our sense of the significance and enormity of sin by relating it to a 'Being', whom we have every reason to love and obey."

Both approaches have their characteristic dangers if not properly understood. The danger is in believing that Christ is so pure and good, and we (humans) are foul and hopeless sinners, thus relapsing into the lowest condition of egoism. This kind of identification with our human condition can take us away from our true (divine) nature. Indeed, in Christian terms, in the Bible, Jesus Christ is reported as saying: "The kingdom of God cometh not with observation. Neither shall they say, lo, here! Or lo, there! For, behold, the kingdom of God is within you" (Luke 17:20–21). Yet, still Christians look to an external divinity. Islam also recognizes that God is not distant from man, with the Koran stating: "We are closer to him than his jugular vein" (Koran 50:16).

As Swami Prabhavananda notes: "The value of the Hindu approach is that it presents the consequences of sin in their ultimate aspect, which is simply alienation from the Reality within us" (Prabhavananda and Isherwood 1953). The danger lies in over-identification with *Atma*, and confusing it with ego. Perhaps the danger of the Hindu approach also lies in its psychological inability to imagine the *Atma* in the way it imagines *Ishwara* (God). It appears that the Hindu approach, too often relapsing into an easy optimism based on the doctrine of reincarnation, takes sins too lightly, believing, as *Atma*, people have millions of lives ahead and sooner or later they will get around to knowing their true nature. On the other hand, perhaps the danger of the Christian approach is exactly the opposite, which stresses the importance of God (*Ishwara*) and minimizes the reality of the in-dwelling *Atma*, of which *Ishwara* is the projection. The value of such dualistic thinking is that it teaches devotion to God, and its danger is that people may tend to exaggerate self-loathing. This over-identification with one's weaknesses could make a person forget their true nature and the obligation it imposes to struggle towards self-knowledge (Prabhavananda and Isherwood 1953).

Abhinavagupta (c. 950–1016 CE), the Kashmiri philosopher and mystic, said that *moksha*, or liberation (from *samsara*, meaning "the circle of death and rebirth") is the awareness of one's true nature (Suresh 2019), meaning the original, innate, pure I-consciousness. The normal psychological I-consciousness is relational (that is, the self-consciousness is in contrast with the not-self). The pure I-consciousness is immediate awareness. When one has this consciousness, one knows one's real nature, and this is what is meant by liberation.

Another point that may be worth mentioning here is, in the East, there appears to be no conflict between religion and science, because science there is not based upon the passion for facts, and religion is not based upon mere faith; there is what is termed "religious cognition" or "cognitive religion." Whereas, in the Western view, the grace of God is everything, in the East, human beings are God, and are believed to have the capacity to redeem themselves. According to the Hindu way, perfect liberation from all impurities can be gained while living here on this earth, whereas in Christianity perfect union with God is possible only in Heaven.

The introverted nature of Hindu religion is well expressed by Swami Vivekananda, who says: "Realization is real religion. . . . You take nothing on trust. You accept nothing but your own experience" (Prabhavanda and Isherwood 1953). It seems, in the East, that religion is sustained by passion and not by intellectual concepts. It is taken as a way of life. In *Religion of Love*, Swami Vivekananda proclaims: "I hope you will always bear in mind this one ideal, that religion is neither in books, nor in intellectual consent, nor in reasoning. Reason, theories, documents, doctrines, books, religious ceremonies, are all helps to religion, religion itself consists of realisation." He adds: "People have been fighting for ages, and what is the outcome? Intellect cannot reach there at all. We have to go beyond the intellect; the proof of religion is in direct perception. . . . it is not learning, but *being*" (Vivekananda 1960).

There is still more that can be said about these differences but, hopefully, these few comparisons well serve the purpose of the research topic. Through religion, spirituality has greatly influenced our way of being. It affects, for example, physical health, coping with illness and death, people's mental well-being, artistic inspiration, various other aspects of culture, and our sense of purpose and meaning. So, how we think, feel, talk, behave, and relate comes from the source of spirituality. Spirituality, perhaps, is the only vital force behind all human actions and inactions.

It would appear to be appropriate to say that Hindu spirituality insists on the validity of experience, while reason is perceived only as a tool for giving expression to the experience. As such, as noted by Meera Sharma and Joseph Ryan in "A Journey of Awakening: The Emergence of Consciousness" in *MOJ Yoga & Physical Therapy*: "No amount of doctrines or philosophy or ethical books you may have stuffed into your brain will matter much; only what you are and what you have realised" (Sharma and Ryan 2018).

## The Current Position of Spiritual Views and Differences

Strangely enough, Indology gave rise to the Western interest in Eastern Vedic scripture. A book by a Dutch missionary to the south of India named Abraham Rogerius, or Abraham Roger (1609–1649) was published in 1651. A Dutch translation of Sanskrit poems about the customs and religion of Brahmins, it was entitled *De Open-Deure tot het verborgen Heydendom ofte Waerachtigh vertoogh van het leven ende zeden, mitsgaders de Religie ende Gotsdienst der Bramines op de Cust Chormandel ende der landen daar ontrent* ("The Open Door to the Hidden Paganism or Truthful Account of Life and Customs, as Well as Religion and Worship of the Brahmins at Coromandel Coast and Surrounding Countries"). Later, an Austrian Roman Catholic priest wrote two Sanskrit grammar texts for the use of Christian missionaries.

In fact, Western interest in India's Vedic scripture was more triggered by reference to the Yajur Veda made by Voltaire (1694–1778) in 1756 in his *Essai sur les Moeurs et l'Esprit des Nations* (translated into English as *An Essay on Universal History, the Manners, and Spirit of Nations*). Later, Warren Hastings (1732–1818), the first Governor-General to India (1773-1785), contributed a good deal towards the development of Indology. He wrote the introduction to the first English translation, in 1785, by Sir Charles Wilkins (1749–1836) of the Bhagavad Gita, and also Hindu codes and laws from ancient scripture.

This opened the gates for Western scholars to study old texts. It appears Germany was also very much influenced by Indology; for example, German philologist and Orientalist Friedrich Max Müller. Similarly, American physicist J. Robert Oppenheimer (1904–1967) was familiar with Hindu philosophy (Hijiya 2000) and, upon contemplating the first atomic explosion, quoted from the *Gita*: "Now I am become Death, the destroyer of worlds" (Temperton 2017). Indeed, the fascination of Adolf Hitler (1889–1945) with "Hindu Tantra" was so great that he made the swastika, ancient symbol of "well-being" or "good fortune," his trademark (Heller 2000). Similarly, he used *abhaya mudrā* (gesture of fearlessness) as his personal hand gesture: the straight-armed Nazi salute (Chandra 2001).

It seems that, until recently, the concepts of Eastern totality have been absent from Western scientific thinking, which focuses on duplicable experiments based on cause and effect, in which one distinct variable at a time can be considered. It appears that for the West, this scientific method seems to be the best way to know anything, which could limit one's perception. Any "oneness" between observer and observed, therefore, was (and, for the most part, still remains) unthinkable and can be labelled as too ridiculous, rather than as in the Eastern view, one would consider it as wisdom beyond thought. Swami Vivekananda, for example, stated in *Pearls of Wisdom*, "All differences in this world are of degree, and not of kind, because oneness is the secret of everything" (Vivekananda 1998).

Whether a person who behaves strangely is defined as mad, ill, or possessed depends on culture. In shamanic cultures, for example, a person's bizarre behaviour (babbling confused words, displaying curious eating habits, singing continuously, dancing wildly, and being tormented by spirits) is an indication that he is an appropriate person to be a shaman, rather than mad.

It would appear, therefore, to be consistent with all previously reported findings to speculate that Western psychology focuses on appearance and seems to avoid knowing the reality behind all appearances, therefore missing the challenge of discovering the one behind the changing many. Indeed, in "Indra's Postmodern Net" in *Philosophy East and West* (Loy 1993) David Loy says that Western philosophy was "largely a search for the one within the many, the Same that grounds Difference"; however, he argues that the 20th century saw "the end of this project: not its realization but its abandonment."

Perhaps Carl Gustav Jung, Swiss psychiatrist and psychoanalyst, was the first person to foresee the differences between the Eastern and Western standpoints, and raised the possibility of each imitating the other. With his understanding and knowledge of the human psyche and the collective unconscious, Jung was concerned about Westerners adopting Eastern values from their usual extroverted position and making dogma out of them, rather than seeking those values within themselves, in their psyches. He believed that the core Eastern teachings consist of an inward-looking mind, which in itself has a self-liberating power. Jung was critical of those Westerners who merely imitated Eastern spirituality superficially and thus risked damage to their psyches. As reported by Radmila Moacanin in *Jung's Psychology and Tibetan Buddhism* (Moacanin 1986), Jung remarked:

> One cannot be too cautious in these matters, for what with the imitative urge and a positively morbid avidity to possess themselves of outlandish feathers and deck themselves out in this exotic plumage, far too many people are misled into snatching at such "magical" ideas—and applying them externally, like an ointment. People will do anything, no matter how absurd, in order to avoid facing their own soul.

Jung's psychology (Singer 1994) may mean different things to different people, but one thing that seems to be appealing (especially if one is a follower of Vedantic philosophy) is that it is not used as a tool, as was the case with many other psychologists of his era.

Jung never seems to have presented a psychological theory in the strict sense of a theory. It appears he had his own unique way of forming intellectual disciplines, drawing from his psychotherapy practice and the prevailing psychological principles available. Based on our admittedly relatively limited knowledge of Jung's work, we note that he did not seem to offer a methodology or a technique of application; rather, his emphasis was on each individual consciously developing a unique philosophy of life. Jung seemed to believe that human beings are born with (given) special personality traits, which unfold in their own time in accordance with "acquired factors."

This philosophy appears to be different from all other Western approaches to the human psyche. In many ways it is similar to Vedic philosophy, which perceives people as unitary and total beings. Jung maintained that, as human beings, we equally possess the opposite quality of what is characteristic in us. It appears to be consistent with his interest in Eastern religions from childhood; therefore, his psychology seems to be influenced by Eastern philosophy. Perhaps, however, he did not explore it enough to give him clarity and security about it, and that is where his confusion lies.

Jung seems to claim that "there is a difference." His study of the feminine and the masculine delved deeply into the unconscious nature of the human psyche. It appears, however, that his work remains limited only to the "gender" level within the realm of psychology, whereas Kundalini yoga prepares one to get to the stage of ultimate union of *purusha* and *prakriti* (masculine and feminine) and even goes a step further, to a stage of pure consciousness, oneness, where the mind dissolves. Perhaps Jung's cultural way of thinking got in his way of understanding the unfolding nature of Eastern philosophy.

He writes in *Psychology and Religion: West and East* (1958):

> This strange antithesis between East and West is expressed most clearly in religious practice. We speak of religious uplift and exaltation; for us God is the Lord of the universe, we have a religion of brotherly love, and in our heaven-aspiring churches there is a *high altar*. The Indian, on the other hand, speaks of *dhyāna*, of self-immersion, and of *sinking* into meditation; God is within all things and especially within man. . . .

While the Westerner attempts to rise above the natural world, the Hindu wishes to sink back into Mother Nature's depths. It is clearly no coincidence that in the first book of the Bible, God says: "Let us make man in our image, after our likeness: and let them have dominion over the fish of the sea, and over the fowl of the air, and over the cattle, and over all the earth, and over every creeping thing that creepeth upon the earth" (Genesis 1:26). Western civilization, therefore, has been based historically on the subjugation of nature.

Certainly, Jung's choice of title for his 1958 work *Psychology and Religion: West and East*, as the book's Editorial Note suggests, is reflective of his opinion that the two religions are widely different. It appears that Ken Wilber, in *No Boundary: Eastern and Western Approaches to Personal Growth* (Wilber 1985), shares Jung's concern about the difference between the Eastern and Western standpoint when he remarks:

> Yet, with all this outbreak of transcendence, most Westerners still have a great deal of difficulty comprehending how it could be that something deep within them which actually transcends space and time, how there could be an awareness within them which, because it transcends the individual, is free of personal problems, tensions and anxieties.

It might be argued, however, that Wilber's Spectrum of Consciousness model, introduced in the book of the same name in 1977 (Wilber 1993), derives not so much from his meditative experiences as from his remarkable far-ranging scholarly review of Perennial Philosophy, encompassing the world's mystical literature, both East and West. Again, however, it is scholarly, yet more theory; the mind seems to be taking over everything, whereas Eastern Vedic scripture is about going beyond the mind.

So far, Jung and Wilber all gained their knowledge of Eastern wisdom from Buddhist sources, though Buddhism itself can be seen as just a narrow branch of Vedic philosophy. Buddhism has three major branches. From earliest times, Buddhism separated into Theravāda ("the Teaching of the Elders" or "the Ancient

Teaching") and Mahāyāna ("the Great Vehicle"). The latter then split between traditional Mahāyāna teachings and Vajrayāna teachings that have an esoteric emphasis. Nevertheless, perhaps it is easier for a Western mind to understand Buddhism with its very structured framework than to enter into the limitless depths of Vedic philosophy. Some people argue that Buddhism is merely reformed Brahminism (or Brahmanism) and that various Buddhist texts can be traced back to Vedic sources (Lindtner 1999). There are, however, some major differences, with Buddhist scriptures carrying "practically no references to the Vedic or any other pre-existing traditions, except negative ones. Their world starts with the Buddha's awakening" (Elst 2002). Indeed, Vedic literature is *apaurusheya* (impersonal), so that various symbols occur (for example, fire or the swastika), but there is no emphasis on a single individual. In marked contrast, as Elst notes, the "central symbol of Buddhism is the Buddha."

Concurrent with present findings, it would appear that the West seems to be more dependent on outward structures; the inner centre is not looked at. Pandit Rajmani Tigunait, successor to Sri Swami Rama as the spiritual head of the Himalayan Institute, says that Indian philosophy utilizes logic to argue points, but that, "Reason only justifies that which intuition or direct experience has revealed" (Tigunait 1983).

As the teachings of the Vedas and Upanishads address the fundamental questions and problems of human life, they transcend the limitations of culture, place, and time. In this way, research into modern consciousness has confirmed the basic thesis of the ancient Indian Upanishads that each person, in the last analysis, is identical with the totality of existence and with the creative principle of the universe. An individual is not just a body-ego but is also the supreme cosmic principle (*Atma-Brahma*). When one adopts such a view of life, then apparent differences do not seem to be threatening for a person's existence.

## *Definitions of Spirituality*

Trying to define spirituality is like trying to count the waves of the ocean—a person cannot count the waves; they can only see and experience them. Similarly, to some extent, one can also talk about one's experience of spirituality. It appears that, in the West, currently the notions about Eastern spirituality are quite mythical. But the true view of Vedic spirituality is not that much different from spirituality in the West. It is like many different roads leading to one destination, just as in the West it is said that, "All roads lead to Rome," which derives from the Latin expression *mille viae ducunt homines per saecula Romam* ("a thousand roads lead men forever to Rome").

According to Ken Wilber, in the West there cannot be a global spirituality unless the perspectives of all sentient beings are taken into account and fully honoured. Wilber says:

> Anybody can say they are being "spiritual"—and they are, because everybody has some type and level of concern. Let us therefore see their actual conception, in thought and action, and see how many perspectives it is in fact concerned with, and how many perspectives it actually takes into account, and how many perspectives it attempts to integrate, and thus let us see how deep and how wide runs that bodhisattva vow to refuse rest until all perspectives whatsoever are liberated into their own primordial nature (Wilber 1997).

Another definition of spirituality comes from Indian author Balasubramanian:

> Spirituality is a disposition, a disciplined way of life through which one can attain spiritual awakening. Usually, it is contrasted with materialistic way of life. The Bhagavad-gītā, the most popular scriptural text of the Hindus, draws a sharp distinction between spiritual and materialistic disposition. It speaks of them as deivi-sampat, i.e. divine nature, and asuri-sampat, i.e. demonic nature, respectively (Balasubramanian 1996).

Both definitions appear to be quite consistent with previously reported findings and clearly show the difference in Eastern and Western thinking. It is just a small example in order to understand how one perceives things according to one's level of consciousness.

This is a very important point towards understanding the purpose of this book, because what Wilber is trying to grapple with is somewhat similar to the way Western scholars have been grappling with the Sanskrit language. It seems they continue thinking in English while looking at a Sanskrit word in front of them. They appear to lack holistic understanding, which somehow initiates collusion with the word.

Popper reminds us that Galileo's character Simplicio is made to say that, "in order to understand Aristotle one must keep every saying of his always before the mind" (Hacking 1975). But perhaps objective knowledge is no longer at all like that. Hal Blacker, editor of the periodical *What is Enlightenment?*, is quoted by Wilber as saying: "All too often, in the translation of the mystical traditions from the East (and elsewhere) into the American idiom, their profound depth is flattened out, their radical demand is diluted, and their potential for revolutionary transformation is squelched" (Wilber 2000).

While trying to bridge this gap, Meera's own understanding of spirituality is very simple. She believes that we are all born with a divine spark (consciousness) within us. We can burn ourselves to ashes when this fire within us is inappropriately used, or we can turn this divine spark into a powerful light to illuminate the universe. We always have a choice. This is where guidance and discipline are needed to put this fire to purposeful use.

This chapter has explored some fundamental spiritual differences between Eastern and Western traditions in order to establish that the basic problem in any one tradition is not the same as in another tradition, due to the influence of culture and language on people's way of thinking. The advantage in understanding those who appear so different from us, however, is that it may help us to understand ourselves more clearly.

The next chapter explores further the role of language and culture, discussing the difficulties in translation from one language to another due to the profound impact of culture on the language. It also investigates the differences that function as barriers in psychotherapy.

Chapter 2

# The Role of Language and Culture

"When I use a word," Humpty Dumpty said in rather a scornful tone, "it means just what I choose it to mean—neither more nor less."

"The question is," said Alice, "whether you can make words mean so many different things."

"The question is," said Humpty Dumpty, "which is to be master—that's all."

—Lewis Carroll (1832–1898),<br>Through the Looking-Glass

## *The Role of Language*

Language is greater than the sum of its parts, and it would be wrong to discuss the parts and mechanisms of language without a wider view of its functions. This chapter looks at language as a whole by examining some of the ways it is used by people generally or by those who specialize in this field. The interrelated relationship of language and culture has immense impact on human development as a whole, but here, only those areas that are relevant to this book are discussed.

Although the purpose of this book does not pertain to the question "What is language?," the idea is to establish some of the facts about the power and depth of language and how it is intertwined with the philosophy, psychology, and spirituality of a particular culture. Meanings of words can be easily distorted when they are not holistically understood. Indeed, there is much more to a language than so far has been discovered by scholars engaged in this field. Like knowledge, if not properly understood, language can be a hindrance in a person's growth, too. It seems to be true in the case of spirituality.

Similarly, the Vedas were not written down for a long time; rather, they were the lived knowledge of individuals passed on through experience. Only *dwijas* ("twice-born") were worthy of receiving the Vedas. *Dwija* means the one who has attained the real innocence of Buddha nature. They have lost their first childhood in knowledge and have become aware of what they have lost. They have lost the precious, the essential for the non-essential, so they drop their knowledge and become innocent again.

The Vedas are said to be about absolute truth, and the absolute can be known only in innocence. It is said that, "Nothing in all creation is hidden from God's sight. Everything is uncovered and laid bare before the eyes of him to whom we must give account" (Hebrews 4:13). We are, therefore, naked before God. So, we are called to drop all barriers in order to see ourselves as we are, and not as we think we are.

The reason it took so long for the Vedas to be written down was that language had to be perfected in order to attempt to hold the immensity of that experience. Once again, during this current age, the ancient wisdom of the Vedas is facing the same challenge of language. This time it is more intense, since translators in the West have very little knowledge of Vedic spiritual traditions, culture, philosophy, and religion. Such Western scholars have been trying to translate the scripture into a foreign language, reducing the meaning to an abstract, and seem to be satisfied with the result.

Before we investigate what lies beneath the surface meaning of the Sanskrit words that Western language is missing, an overview of language development in the Western world may be helpful. It is easy to get lost in the vastness of this subject, so we will keep the focus on areas that are relevant to this discussion.

Modern linguists seem to have done a good job when it comes to the surface meanings of words. William S. Y. Wang (b. 1933–) puts this clearly in *The Emergence of Language Development and Evolution* (Wang 1991) when he says that no matter how we have fashioned the language to our needs, language has made us who we are.

The emergence of language draws from many specializations. Biologists examine the different levels of communication and how it developed over a period of time across several species. Archaeologists suggest that language written, as well as spoken, could have one origin and over centuries spread globally. Linguists discuss society's contribution towards the development and creation of new languages, whereas psychologists explore the cognitive and physiological mechanisms of language and dysfunction resulting from impairments of these mechanisms. Interesting issues around class and gender have also emerged from these claims. For example, in his 1986 book *An Introduction to Language and Society*, Martin Montgomery states that men and women develop within two different subcultures. He concludes that men and women do not share the same communicative competence. Due to their different patterns of socializing in two different subcultures, their rule system for the use of interpretation of utterances is quite different. It is interesting to note that this could mean that the same text translated by different genders may communicate different messages.

According to Wang (1991), Indo-European languages are related. The traditional view of the spread of the Indo-European languages suggests that an Ur-language was spoken by nomadic horsemen who lived in western Russia near the North Sea at the beginning of the Bronze Age. These mounted warriors roamed over and conquered other countries and imposed their own proto-Indo-European language on them.

Wang maintains that the starting point of the problem of the origins of Indo-European language is not so much archaeological but linguistic. Linguists can quickly perceive that the languages of Europe are related. The connection can be seen in vocabulary, grammar, and phonology. To illustrate the relatedness in vocabulary, he compares the words for the numbers one to 10 in several Indo-European languages. This comparison clarified significant similarities among many European languages, and also Sanskrit, the language of the old Indian literary texts, but languages such as Chinese or Japanese did not fit in the same family.

This is known as *Die Stammbaumtheorie* (Family Tree theory), which was introduced by a German philologist called August

Schleicher (1821–1868) in the 1850s. Sir Monier Monier-Williams (1819–1899), author of *A Sanskrit-English Dictionary* (Monier-Williams 1899), points out that all European alphabets are really Asiatic and not European in their origin, and maintained that certain features of European alphabets connect them to the Devanagari alphabet of the Brahmins, although numerous accessory appliances of European alphabets (such as capital and small letters, brackets, full stops, hyphens, and so on) make them better suited than any other graphic system to meet the linguistic requirements of today.

The dominant linguistic group in northern Africa is the Afro-Asiatic, which includes ancient Egyptian and the Berber languages, as well as the Semitic group, which are supposed to have originated in Arabia. Wang says research by linguist David McAlpin of the University of London reveals that the ancient language Elamite is related to the Dravidian languages of India (McAlpin 1974, 1975). Although still controversial, these findings are remarkably supportive in establishing a close linguistic and genetic relationship among the ancestral languages of the Indo-European, Afro-Asiatic, and Dravidian groups, which were quite close together in the Near East about 10,000 years ago.

These claims concerning language are quite relevant. Firstly, they confirm the role of culture in the formation of a language and, secondly, the symbolic importance of language. Symbols are like the tip of the iceberg—the major part of them remains unknown and unconscious. Moreover, they are archetypical and thus, mean different things to different people. Finally, linguistic investigations only go back 10,000 years, whereas Vedic scripture may have existed before that time, initially orally and then later in a fully developed and alive language, Sanskrit.

Similarly, among Buddhists, the early teachings of the Buddha were not written down but chanted in groups. Sōtō Zen monk Brad Warner (b. 1964) speculates that perhaps adherents were "suspicious of the written word's ability to carry on the real spirit of the teaching. Or maybe it was because literacy wasn't so widespread then and they figured an oral transmission had a better chance of surviving" (Warner 2019). Legend has it that Veda

Vyāsa ("the one who classified the Vedas" or the "splitter of the Vedas") compiled the primordial single Veda into four collections, helping people to understand better the divine knowledge contained within them (Wikipedia: Vyasa 2020). Later, the Upanishads encapsulated some of the primary spiritual concepts and teachings of the Vedas.

Again, systemic linguistics represent language as a series of systems, each system being a set of options available to a speaker, or writer, in a given social environment. They attach high priority to social functions, and are particularly interested in registers and dialects. Language is complex—more complex than even the crude procedures suggested above do justice to it.

In *Outline of Linguistic Analysis*, Bernard Bloch and George L. Trager (Bloch and Trager 1942) defined language as "a system of arbitrary vocal symbols by means of which a social group cooperates." J. F. Wallwork, in *Language and Linguistics: An Introduction to the Study of Language* (Wallwork 1969), stresses the symbolic nature of language. He points towards the danger of identification with the object if the symbolic nature is overlooked. Wallwork clearly suggests that, when people use symbols differently, confusion persists.

This concept of the power of symbols is beautifully expressed in a few words by Thomas Carlyle (1795–1881) in *Sartor Resartus* ("The Tailor Re-tailored"), his philosophical novel (Carlyle 1831): "For is not a Symbol ever, to him who has eyes for it, some dimmer or clearer revelation of the Godlike?" Indeed, he suggests that "the Universe is but one vast Symbol of God; nay if thou wilt have it, what is man himself but a Symbol of God" and notes the "mystic god-given force" that is in humans.

Metaphors, like symbols, are the tip of the iceberg—what remains unseen is the source and cause of its existence. The same is likely true in the case of language and culture. According to Nigel Pennick in *Magical Alphabets* (Pennick 1992), the very basis of language is metaphorical. He says that alphabets "are one of the most highly sophisticated means by which we humans can try to gain some understanding of the world, and our place within it."

Pennick continues his argument by saying that properly created alphabets from ancient times are all metaphorical. Of course, in their essential nature, languages are metaphorical, as they represent objects in the world or ideas in people's minds, while not being these objects or ideas. Frequently, people choose something from their past experience to describe something else that may be similar to it in some way, and may use an anthropocentric comparison.

So, for example, Pennick says: "We speak of a body of water, a body of work, even a body of men. We speak of the head of a bed, a table, a page, a nail. . . . A clock has a face, just as does a playing card, a rock. . . . Weapons are called arms. A race or a contest may be divided into a number of legs. . . . and so forth" (Pennick 1992). He concludes, therefore, that a great deal of language sees the external world through metaphors of already known objects, especially those relating to the various parts of the human body. This is not a static process, hence new words are formed whenever required.

Pennick also points out that the metaphorical nature of language is manifested philosophically within the concept of man as the microcosm, which is at the very basis of esoteric thinking in the Western world. This is encapsulated in the Hermetic maxim "as above, so below," which is found in the *Emerald Tablet of Hermes*, sometimes ascribed to the mythological Egyptian founder of science, Hermes Trismegistus (Internet Sacred Text Archive, n.d.). This insightful understanding of reality also states that which is below is actually a reflection of that which is above, "As below, so above" (Internet Sacred Text Archive, n.d.). The microcosm of the human being reflects, and is also a part of, the wider world that we refer to as the macrocosm or universe.

As Pennick notes, this reflection exists at every possible level, and "the way things happen" is a phenomenological pattern. It is by the recognition of these patterns and their meaning that it is possible to gain an insight into the nature of reality. When people take a deep look at themselves, therefore, it is possible for them to realize that "we are replicas of the universe" (Sharma and Ryan 2014).

As shown previously, it may be deduced from the study of Western linguists that the extrovert nature of Western philosophy and spirituality is prevalent in their research of language. At some point, however, they come to a halt, much in the same way as in a psychotherapy practice a therapist feels stuck with their clients' issues when the same is not resolved within the practitioner. Therapists can only go along with their clients as far as they have taken themselves in their own growth process, and it is only possible to work with what we know. It would appear, therefore, that words used in Western languages are limited in their depth of meaning. In the Sanskrit language, for example, there are numerous words for "one thing"—air, fire, water, moon, sun, river, or ocean; everything has 30 to 50 different names, possibly more. The words were formed to fit into the inner reality of a person.

As an example, in "The Subjective View of Life 'Evenness of Mind is Yoga. Equanimity Within is Spiritual Life' (Gita: 2–48)" in *MOJ Yoga & Physical Therapy*, Meera Sharma writes that the word *prabhāt* means:

> . . . . rising, innocent, baby-like sun that is just emerging from the dark womb of the night. It is associated with new beginnings, more so as it has spiritual associations with the meaning of awakening and light of consciousness rising in one's inner horizon, a time for salutation to one's eternal nature. This word *prabhat* is only meant for the moment the sun rises; it cannot be used for midday or noon sun. There are different names for the sun for other timings. There is a word for "sunrise" (*suryodyā*) that is understood more in theoretical terms. But *prabhāt* has a more experiential, spiritual and phenomenological sense to it. It is changeable and different from one day to another. Like in the English language the word "dawn" is for the rising sun; that is the sun of the day. But *prabhāt* contains in it the energy of the uniqueness of that moment as its capacity of creation of cosmic light, a birthing time, a new beginning. It is not the sun of the day; the sun is different at different times of the day. But some-

how these words appear to give a sense of external surface and correspond with the extrovert nature of the West (Sharma 2017a).

Unsurprisingly, English Orientalist and professor of Hindustani John Shakespear (1774–1858) translated *prabhāt* simply as "morning" or "dawn" (Shakespear 1817).

On the other hand, the word *sandhya* means "descending sun, merging into darkness." Actually, the word *sandhi* means "union," a meeting point of *purusha* (consciousness) and *prakriti* (unconsciousness), animus and anima, where procreation takes place, time dominated by ever-changing *prakriti*; again, a time for salutations to one's inner union with nature.

Both sunrise and sunset are considered to be spiritually very powerful times and are meditated upon. Many rituals and ceremonies are associated with them. *Ravi* is the adolescent sun, also associated with knowledge and *prana* (breath, life force, or vital principle), whereas *suřya* is related to the powerful youth and adult nature of the sun as it makes its journey during daytime towards night. *Ruddrah* is also a name used for the sun in a purely spiritual sense, which means the deity that is responsible for manifestation, maintenance of manifestation, and withdrawal of manifestation of the world process; the souls that have evolved to the status of realization of Shiva (or Siva) consciousness (supreme Consciousness).

A culturally aware person may have a philosophical understanding of these words and, just by using the correct word at the right place in the construction of a sentence, is able to unfold the innermost knowledge and understanding of the reality of that moment. Meera recounts that:

> It was a painful experience when recently my friend's father died, and I was asked to say a few words of homage to him at his funeral. My speech was in Hindi, and it took me less than two minutes to read it out. Everyone was deeply moved by the depth of what was said. People were so impressed that they requested me to translate it into English. I felt utterly disappointed at my inability

to translate the actual meaning of the original text. The message was not coming across in the same way.

It is important to notice that the construction of a sentence in Sanskrit, Prakrit (which was used for a thousand years, from the 4th–5th century BCE to the 8th century CE [Venkatesh 2018]), and even in Hindi is quite different from the English language. When translated into English, it loses that poetic elasticity, aliveness, and depth that makes it so graceful. Indeed, the great Sanskrit grammarian, Pānini (fl. 4th century BCE), repeatedly emphasized the formation of a sentence, as well as accentuation of words, in order to get the correct knowledge and meaning of Sanskrit words.

Since this chapter explores Sanskrit words and their meanings and distortions by Western scholars, it is important to explain here how Sanskrit may be understood. (For details on translations of Sanskrit words, please see the Glossary.)

Sanskrit means the learned language of India, the language of its cultured inhabitants—the language of its literature, religion, and science (Monier-Williams 2011). It represents the learned form of the language brought by the Indian branch of the great Aryan race into India. This assumption is based on the fact that the course of the development of the Sanskrit language in India resembles the course of the Aryan languages in other countries, in similar circumstances. As the language of the Aryan race prevailed over that of the aboriginal people, it separated into two lines. The one taken by the educated and learned classes is known as Aryan, and the other by the unlearned is known as Unaryan.

Due to the very strong influence and power of Indian priests, who wanted to keep the key of knowledge in their possession, the language of the learned classes became highly elaborated. To denote its superiority to the common dialects (*Prakrita*) and its more exclusive dedication for religious and literary purpose, it received the name *Samskrita*, meaning perfectly constructed speech or holistic (absolute) speech. Comparing between the principle members of the Aryan family, Sanskrit is the eldest sister and English one of the youngest. Sanskrit, as a guardian of old Indo-European forms, exhibits remarkable properties better than any other members of the Aryan line of speech.

Monier-Williams (2011), in *A Sanskrit-English Dictionary*, writes that such a book must not be tried by ordinary laws, for Sanskrit has developed more than Greek and German, and any other Aryan language of the world. The love of composition is one of the most characteristic features of Sanskrit, because ancient scripture consists entirely of hymns. Sanskrit as a language was perfected by the old sages of India to enable it to contain within the mirror reflection of their spiritual experiences.

## *The Role of Culture*

When people generally talk about Eastern culture, it appears that they are mainly talking about Indian culture, although China can also be included for its similarities with Indian culture. Somehow, however, Indian culture seems to be more uniquely recognizable than other Eastern cultures. Since culture has a deep impact on language, it is best to explore the factors causing the distinction between Eastern and Western cultures. It can be said that culture is the measuring rod of a civilization.

The difference between an uncivilized, barbarous country and a civilized state lies in their cultures. Defining a culture, Balmiki Prasad Singh (b. 1942), the 14th Governor of Sikkim (2008–2013), India, says in *India's Culture: The State, the Arts and Beyond* that:

> when a set of people live for a long period of time in a particular geographical area, respecting certain philosophical values and virtues of life, there emanates an aroma which is known as culture. All these aspects are common to all different countries, just as the heads, the trunk and the limbs are common to all human beings although they may differ in shape, size and colour (Singh 1998).

It has been suggested that the values respected by people are greatly influenced by the external exigencies of life. From this perspective, geography, climate, and environment may play a great role in determining the first age of civilization. Once culture is shaped and determined by values, as Singh (1998) notes, the external environment does not have the same influence over the culture.

It may be argued that the land in Western countries was rugged and hard because of severe climatic conditions, including snowfall and ice; consequently, the people became tough. For their self-preservation, they had to train themselves to fight unrelenting nature and acquire what they needed from her. Thus, the conquest of nature became a fundamental trait in the character of Western people. On the other hand, the land in the East yielded in abundance, and spring-like weather flourished nearly nine months of the year. This harmony with nature is expressed everywhere in life, and a culture developed based upon "serving and giving" instead of "fighting and procuring." Thus, in the East, a culture emerged from peace, tranquillity, and love, whereas in the West, materialism took root with the idea of conquest.

Civilizations flourish with the promotion of culture; the reverse is also true, as in the fall of the Egyptian, Greek, and Roman empires. When a culture deteriorates, there is an increase in barbarity and immorality in the country and its philosophy is misinterpreted, leading to confusion and chaos among its people. It may be argued that this, more or less, is what is happening world-wide at present, and that this is the age of *Kali Yuga*, at the end of which the world will be destroyed. From a spiritual perspective, however, this is the time to arrest the deterioration by reviving the great philosophical and religious values of life.

Indian culture, with its own unbroken history, has gradually developed over the ages. The roots of Indian culture go beyond that of the Aryans to the Negritos, who came to India from Africa, the Aboriginals who belonged to the proto-Australoid race, the Mongoloids who came from Tibet and China, and the Dravidians inhabiting southern India. Aryans alone were not the conquerors of this land. Later came the Greeks, followed by the Shakas and the Kushanas. Before and during King Gupta's time came Hans followed by the Turks. In Assam, the Ahoms of the Shan race of Upper Burma arrived and settled down for good. In fact, all the communities that came to India before the Muslims lost their identity by assimilating into the existing society. Poet and musician Rabindranath Tagore (1861–1941) summed it up beautifully when he said that all the people who came to India mingled with one another to become one living organism: *Ek deho holo lin* (Singh 1998).

Although Muslims were able to maintain a separate identity, their social habits and customs became highly affected by the prevailing culture of India, and so did their language and the language of Indians. The current spoken and written language, Hindi, is very different from the pre-Muslim Prakrit language of India. Present Hindi consists of many Arabic and Urdu words, and carries with it Muslim cultural and philosophical impressions. The same is true in the case of Urdu spoken by Indian Muslims, which is quite different from its original form, known as Arabic.

The arrival of Europeans in India also brought far-reaching changes in India's cultural heritage. It seems that the restlessness of the European spirit was trying to bring everything under its control. With the introduction of Western capitalism and technology, the material conditions also underwent a huge change, whereas Christianity with its international character emerged as yet another religion on the Indian scene. Indeed, according to Robert Eric Frykenberg (2008) in *Christianity in India: From Beginnings to the Present*, tradition intimates that the Apostle Thomas arrived in India around 52 CE. This suggestion, however, is subject to dispute and to "identify, trace, or validate the baffling array of source materials relating to Christian origins in India is a complex task."

Centuries later, the introduction of English in the existing educational system was momentous. Although according to *The British in India: Three Centuries of Ambition and Experience* (Gilmour 2018), the aim was to provide more English-speaking administrators to manage India, commonly referred to as the "jewel in the crown" of the British Empire, the consequences were far more significant. Books translated and written in the English language exposed Indian scripture to the rest of the world, where new ideas about democracy, nationalism, and scientific development emerged.

Thus, it appears that Indian people are neither purely Aryan nor Dravidian, but are a mixture of all the great people who came and made India their home. Today's Indian culture is a blend of all these elements. Chaudhuri, in *Hinduism: A Religion to Live By* (1962), says that by the year 1 CE, India was a highly developed culture. The cultural attainments of India can be viewed in the context of language and literature, religion and spirituality, visual and performing arts, economics, philosophy, and science.

Civilization may have developed in India over five millennia ago. This is suggested by the legends and myths of the subcontinent, together with archaeological evidence of ancient pottery, agricultural tools, and the native handicrafts that survived through the ages. According to Balmiki Prasad Singh in "Understanding India," in the journal *Dialogue* (2006), such a stable base provided the opportunity for people to study the fine arts and delve into philosophical enquiry. The beginnings of Indian literature found in the Vedic hymns, both prose and poetry, were composed exclusively in Devanagari Sanskrit and handed down orally. Pali, Prakrit, and Sanskrit are known as Aryan languages. The earliest Dravidian language was Tamil. Both Pali and Prakrit were the languages of the masses.

Singh (2006) notes that, considering India's long past, it is worth remembering that we are dealing with a culture that has sustained a highly individualistic ethos and a stratified society. The traditional Indian society gradually became hierarchical both in principle and in practice. It developed institutions of caste and untouchability. Religion was reduced to caste and communal mores. The caste system broke up the unity of Indian life and impeded the growth of democracy. These factors have hindered the development of an open society. Again, the colonial ethos was the major force that, in spite of educational development, perpetrated the distinction between people according to status. All this narrowed the social life to a great degree and still persists to some extent.

At present, India is going through a rather acute crisis in the domain of cultural consciousness. For instance, extended family systems are disappearing, the educational system is becoming more Westernized, and the old values and traditions no longer have the same place in modern society. The traditions, which once facilitated a generation of creative persons who revitalized Indian cultural responses to pressing problems of the day, have declined.

Western technology has also contributed towards social change, and "culture shock" is the consequence. This occurs, as American writer and futurist Alvin Toffler (1928–2016) describes in *Future Shock* (1970), when the accelerative change in a society goes beyond the ability of a person to adapt to it.

Singh (1998) argues, regardless of Eastern or Western differences, culture is about the norms and values that are held by various groups in society. It is about similarities and differences in things such as language, style of expression, dress, and a whole way of life that is passed from generation to generation. Culture allows us to separate one group of people from another on the basis of their distinctive patterns of behaviour. It is often taken for granted. Wherever people go, they take their culture with them, which gives a sense of belonging, particularly when with others of their own culture. The problem arises when a person is with others from a different culture who think that their culture is superior and that there is something wrong with those who do not share their norms and values. There is a tendency for individuals to make a judgement about others based on their own cultural norms and values. If people are to relate effectively with those of another culture, they will need to be more open and accepting of diversity.

In a way, culture is power. As expressed through language and art, philosophy and religion, education and science, films and newspapers, radio and television, customs and social habits, economic organizations and political institutions, culture heightens the skills of an individual—and a society in its totality—in all walks of life. Perhaps it is by culture that a person or a society gets insight into the whole. Singh suggests that culture not only includes art, dance, drama, and music but a whole way of life. In a broader sense, culture is *sanskriti*, or "a process of refinement."

Regardless of Eastern or Western perspectives, therefore, it seems obvious that there is a growing acceptance of the role of language and culture in the evolution of human development. It is not only in language that spirituality and religion express themselves; it is also in the material expression of culture. In both these ways, spirituality plays a balancing role in shaping a path of development in line with world development trends. As such, culture and language constitute both a balancing and a driving force of development, and an objective of development itself.

Above all else, culture and language contribute towards maintaining a quality of natural environment, and a sense of dignity and self-confidence. It can be argued that there would be neither sustainable economic growth nor social progress and durable peace, if growth of culture and language was not maintained in tune with people's heritage. The role of culture and language, therefore, in the maintenance and development of any society cannot be taken lightly. Both culture and language have contributed towards the acceleration of people's conduct and belief systems over a long history. Although the conceptual distinction between culture and language is valid to some extent, its interdependence needs adequate emphasis. The need to establish this interrelationship between culture and language seems imperative to bridge the gap between what people say and what they do.

According to Singh, when anything is translated into another language without taking into consideration the cultural impact and influence of what has been translated, then the original meaning is not conveyed or communicated; instead, a new meaning is created. Due to a lack of understanding of interrelationships between culture and language, the result is an unwelcome compromise. As Ken Wilber observes in *One Taste: Daily Reflections on Integral Spirituality* (2000): "The reason is that if translation is too quickly, or too abruptly, or too ineptly taken away from an individual (or a culture), the result, once again, is not breakthrough but breakdown, not release but collapse."

In the introduction to *A Sanskrit-English Dictionary* (1899), Sir Monier Monier-Williams also confirms the same, when he says that knowledge gained by his personal contact with Indian Pandits and educated men, as well as with all sorts of traditions, and the condition of Hindus in their towns and villages, was a distinct advantage in his work compiling the dictionary. He further adds that this philosophical understanding enabled him to avoid many mistakes made by other Sanskritists who possessed only book knowledge of India. He also emphasizes the indispensable nature of accents in the Sanskrit language, without which knowledge of the correct meaning of Sanskrit words is lost. In fact, the whole of Pānini's grammar is interpenetrated throughout by the ruling idea of the importance of accentuation to the correct knowledge and pronunciation (even the accent, pitch, and tone matters) of words and their meanings.

Colin Lago and Joyce Thompson, in *Race, Culture and Counselling* (1996), note that language is socially transmitted and imbued with cultural mores and beliefs. These have a deep impact and effect upon people's ways of viewing and thinking of their world. Also affected is their understanding of the relationships they have with others, objects, and occurrences in their lives, as well as what they feel is worth pursuing.

It must also be remembered that, as Joseph Ryan in "Photography as a Tool of Awareness" in *Journal of Transpersonal Psychology* (2012) writes, "The way things are seen is a reflection of a person's being." This can be seen, for example, in the psychological phenomenon of projection. In 12-step programmes, it is often encapsulated in the phrase, "If you spot it, you got it" (Zamonski et al. 2013), meaning that if you see something in others then you have it within yourself, too.

It appears that every culture has a tendency to create, and is supported by, what Lago and Thompson call a "basic personality type," and this is "composed of the complex personality characteristics" in a specific culture. During the middle of the 20th century, Americans Benjamin Whorf (1897–1941) and Edward Sapir (1884–1939) suggested that there was a close relationship between thought and language. According to Edward T. Hall in *Beyond Culture* (1989), Whorf's greatest contribution to thinking in the West was "his meticulous descriptions of the relationship of language to events in a cross-cultural context. He demonstrated that cultures have unique ways of relating language to reality. . . . Nothing happens in the world of humans that is not deeply influenced by linguistic forms." Thus, Lago and Thompson surmise that if it is true that language and thought are related closely to each other, it follows that there is also a close link between language and experience.

As language follows thought, then how people think about their experiences will be guided by the opportunities or constraints offered by the language of their culture. Edward Sapir, in *Conceptual Categories in Primitive Languages* (1931) has suggested that it "actually defines experience for us by reason of its formal completeness and because of our unconscious projection of its implicit expectations into the field of experience.... Such categories such as number, gender, case, tense, mode, voice, 'aspect' and a host of others .... are not so much discovered in experience as imposed upon it...."

Language, then, potentially shapes and limits experience. Is then a particular experience available to someone who does not have the words to define it? Roger W. Brown pointed out in 1956 that much experience can be differentiated in one language's lexicon but be undifferentiated in that of another. One example would be the perception of colour in different cultures. The languages of the Pacific Islands fail to distinguish between the colours blue and green, and the Native American Navajo Nation only has a single word for brown and green. In contrast, there is a considerable range of words for types of snow in arctic and subarctic regions. In Scotland, for example, which is noted for cold and inclement winter weather, there are numerous words for snow, such as: feefle (to swirl), flindrikin (a slight snow shower), skelf (a large snowflake), snaw-pouther (fine driving snow), and spitters (small drops or flakes of wind-driven rain or snow) (BBC 2015).

Experience, emotion, and meaning are all linked with language, but this may be stretched when it comes to subjects that are abstract in nature, according to Lago and Thompson. If two people look at an object, such as a vase, then it is possible to assume that there is a shared common perceptual experience in the statement, "I see a vase." Where there is no outside solid reference, however (for example, when somebody declares, "I feel distressed"), then assuming a common experience between people cannot be certain, particularly when translating from one language to another. This is known as a "nominalization," for example, depressed, happy, sad, and so on.

This is potentially hazardous when translated across cultures, where attempts to create mutual understanding can lead to a host of inadequate approximations or, at worst, an incorrect appreciation of the meaning that is intended to be conveyed. This is due to the lack of external references to the topic in question. The emotional states have to be "imagined" by the recipient of the message.

Colin Lago (2006) describes how Dr. J. Maw, in a 1980 lecture, reported initial difficulties with understanding African students, who presented with various complaints to British student health services, including itching sensations in the head or stomach aches. African medical colleagues, when consulted, suggested that the students might be suffering anxiety or depression. The direct translation into English provided a somatic interpretation rather than an emotional one.

Edward T. Hall (1976) has used a notion called "extension transference," which, as a theoretical concept, describes language as a symbolization of something that happened, is happening, or will happen. Language in its written form is an extension of the spoken form and, therefore, is "a symbolization of symbolization!" This extension may become either confused with the process described, or even take its place (Lago and Thompson 1996).

This process appears to blend with the hypothesis put forward by Leff in 1973 of "a scheme for the historical development of words denoting emotional states. Where previously one word may have existed to denote a pattern of physiological response, it is likely that that word came to denote an emotional state or experience as well as the somatic condition. The focus of meaning subsequently shifted to the experiencing of emotion and the somatic meaning faded into the background" (Lago and Thompson 1996).

In other words, an extension transference has taken place. In the continuing development of the word, it is likely that it became split up into phonetically related variants as the global interpretation was differentiated into several smaller categories. Lago and Thompson note that the relationship between language, thought, and experience is, therefore, extremely complex. Also, this implies that thought and experience are subject to language. Hence, when learning about other cultures, there are clear language limitations when attempting translations of meaning.

It is evident from the long history of culture and language that they have an old and enduring relationship. One facilitating another, even in the very remote areas of human development, they have led to the presence of unique and gifted personalities, art, and architecture at different periods of time. These experiences have influenced people and allowed them to educate themselves in terms of their beliefs and customs, history, religion, and values.

Currently, fears are being expressed about the future of creative diversity, which is now being witnessed through the media revolution, advancing industrial technologies, and global communication networks. This has generated apprehension about rapid Westernization, which will eclipse many ways of living and could even lead to the "Clash of Civilizations," a hypothesis from the 1990s that future conflict would be between cultures rather than countries: "The fault lines between civilizations will be the battle lines of the future" (Huntingdon 1993).

Perhaps this is an exceptional time in the history of humankind, which calls for exceptional solutions. Science and modern technology have reduced distances between people not only physically and globally but on many other levels of communication. As the world is shrinking and turning into a universe as a family, there is greater need for a common language and common culture.

## The Changed Meaning of Sanskrit Words

"In the beginning was the Word, and the Word was with God, and the Word was God. The same was in the beginning with God" (John 1:1–2). This Bible statement is remarkably similar to a verse from the Rig Veda: "In the beginning was Brahman, with whom was the Word; and the Word was truly the supreme Brahman" (Prabhavananda and Isherwood 1953).

The philosophy of the Word may be traced in its various forms and modifications from the ancient Vedic scriptures through the teachings of Plato (428/427–348/347 BCE) and the Stoics to Philo of Alexandria (c. 20 BCE–c. 50 CE) and the author of the Fourth Gospel, traditionally attributed to St John the Apostle (c. 6–c. 100 CE). Perhaps an actual historical link can be proved to exist between all these succeeding schools of thought. It appears that the power of the Word has been recognized by humankind since the dawn of history.

It can be inferred that an alphabet is a system of writing that expresses a language's basic sounds by means of single characters. Historically, there is a common aspect to several of the esoterically based alphabets: each character is assigned a name, which is symbolically representative of an object or a specific quality (Pennick 1992).

This can be described in the example of the word *akash* ("sky"), where each letter within the word has its own source of power. This idea is present to a sophisticated degree in early medieval Celtic oghams, the Nordic runes, and in Greek. Culturally, the concept may come from the phonetic alphabet, which is believed to have originated in ancient Egypt. Also, however, it may be due to assimilating earlier pictographs into the newly developing alphabets (Pennick 1992).

Unlike many other culturally bound esoteric traditions (Pennick 1992), the Jewish Kabbalah is based on an inner visionary experience and expresses direct access to the knowledge of a powerful magical alphabet. The art of gematria is an important part of sacred alphabet symbolism, where every word written in Greek letters is then changed into a corresponding number (Pennick 1992). The same is followed in the Hebrew tradition. Sanskrit is similar, in that words generating from yogic tantra also are based on sacred geometry.

In all ancient languages, esoteric thought is common, and magical alphabets have a special function in enabling the seeker to experience the transformative processes. They are intended to help people delve further than the mere external in order to explore deeper meanings of reality. As such, they can convey meanings that are impossible to communicate in other ways (Pennick 1992).

According to Vedic scripture, the Goddess Kali wears a gruesome garland of 50 human skulls, which is called the *varnamālā* ("the Garland of Letters"). Each skull represents a letter of the alphabet. Elizabeth Harding (1993) says that the Garland of Letters illustrates the universe of names and forms; that is, speech (*sabda*) and its meaning or object (*artha*). Each letter is called an *akshara*, meaning "imperishable" or "immutable." When they are combined, *aksharas* become words that are expressed orally. Each of the *aksharas*, however, also has a male and female deity and, by their union, creation can evolve.

Kali is sound—the sound that created this universe. All knowledge is embedded in its name and form changes, but sound remains. As stated by the ancient sages, three-quarters of this sound remains unmanifested within ordinary human beings. As Kapil Deva Dvivedi (1990) states in *The Essence of the Vedas* (1990), the only audible part is the gross sound, manifested daily through our mouths.

As noted by John M. Koller in *Asian Philosophies*, speech is "among the auspicious powers symbolized as deities in the Vedas" (Koller 2017). So, Vac ("speech") is the goddess of communication. Koller also notes that speech "provides a way of controlling things by giving them names. Knowledge, the most powerful means of controlling existence that human beings have, is essentially vac, consciousness operating through speech."

Indo-European languages branched from the root of Sanskrit are said to be the Goddess Kali's invention. As Robert Graves writes in *The White Goddess: A Historical Grammar of Poetic Myth* (Graves 2010), Kali created the esoteric letters of the Sanskrit alphabet and inscribed them on the rosary of skulls around her neck. The letters were magic because they stood for primordial creative energy expressed in sound, in her holy language. In short, Kali's worshippers originated the doctrine of the logos, or creative words, which later on were adopted by Christians and the West.

Similarly, in the Hebrew language, which is one of the sacred languages of the world (others being Arabic, Greek, Latin, and Sanskrit), there are three classes of letters in the alphabet: aspirates, mutes, and sibilants. In the Hebrew alphabet (Pennick 1992), after these three "mothers," the seven doubles are most important. They symbolize the pair of opposites that compose existence and signify two phonetic values: a sound that is hard and one that is soft. They also symbolize the seven directions: north, south, east, and west, above, below, and centre. According to the *Sefer Yetzirah* (the Jewish *Book of Creation*), it was God who formed the seven planets and the days of the week from these letters (Pennick 1992; Sparavigna 2014).

On the microcosmic level, the "gates of the soul" (corresponding to the seven ancient known planets) originated from these letters. They are the two eyes, ears, and nostrils and the single mouth. The tradition of the bard in Wales also contains the idea of the universe originating from three "mother" letters (Pennick 1992), with bardic music described in *The Lore of the Bard: A Guide to the Celtic & Druid Mysteries* as "a twin of poetry, a secret language of the soul" (Rowan 2003). It is evident, therefore, that the power of "word" is much more than existing modern measuring techniques are capable of conceiving. Only with an altered state of consciousness is it possible to dive into the depth of these words.

There are, however, perhaps other factors. As Edward E. Smith and Douglas L. Medin put it in *Concepts and Categories* (1981):

> Without concepts, mental life would be chaotic. If we perceived each entity as unique, we would be overwhelmed by the sheer diversity of what we experience and unable to remember more than a minute fraction of what we encounter. And if each individual entity needed a distinct name, our language would be staggeringly complex and communication virtually impossible.

This perhaps gives a clear indication of the difference between the Eastern and Western construction of language. In the West, the way to simplify a complex world, full of individuality and variation, has been to group objects and events together on the basis of some similarity between them. The process of grouping words together is termed "categorization." The end product of this process is often termed "a concept." For the Westerner, this way of categorizing experience, involving the use of concepts, may be an important way of simplifying the world.

In order to learn from experience, humans need to be able to recognize similarity and difference. Objects can be grouped together at various levels of abstraction. In a chapter entitled "The Genesis of Higher Mental Functions" in *Cognitive Development to*

*Adolescence* (1988), Lev Semyonovich Vygotsky (1896–1934) identifies two separate roles of language: as a means of communication and as the basis of thought. The language of a culture is likely to be closely involved in the conceptual development of the people within that culture.

In the East, a "concept" or word having meaning is drawn from an experiential realization of experience that is holistic in nature. For example, when Meera looks up and see the sky, she relates to it as *akash*. It fills her with a sense of unity with *akash*. She is joined with *akash*, and immediately she is aware of the qualities of it as her own energetic qualities. A communication is established between the two, despite the distance. In a mystical manner, it can be referred to as a "journey of no distance," or a level of communication between frequencies. Her physical energy centres open up to experience this non-verbal communication. First of all, however, she has to have a knowledge and understanding of the meaning of the word *akash* and what it means to her philosophically. An absence of such an understanding would limit her experience.

Further to Meera's experience of *akash*, and to clarify it in general expression, we can say that different languages embody different forms of understanding. On this score, Ben-Ami Scharfstein (1978) raises some interesting points. Perhaps the most striking is the way he views these "different forms of understanding" as crucial to the development of comparative philosophy. Talking about the uniqueness of each language, he notes:

> Those who accept it say that a language is not simply a neutral medium in which to think and communicate. Its structure, they say, is its own, its vocabulary makes unique distinctions, it has its own method of combining word-fractions and words, it has its own parts of speech (if it has them at all), and it expresses temporal relations in its own way. Furthermore, its lilts and sounds have their own peculiarly aesthetic nature. . . . It is in agreement with such a view that a French expert in the languages of Africa has claimed that the scientific study of these languages requires "radical cultural adjustment." Europeans, he writes,

have mistakenly tried to read their grammar into non-European languages (Scharfstein 1978).

In a spiritual (esoteric) sense, the way Meera relates to the word *akash* is very much the same as what the Buddhist Madhyamika text says about the significance of language. As the Dalai Lama writes in *Beyond Dogma: The Challenge of the Modern World* (1996), the meaning of words does not evolve without control; most often it is linked to the intention of the user, an intention that depends, among other things, on the context and the frame of reference. This may be why *akash* will not necessarily mean the same thing to a Westerner, depending on the user and the context and moment of its use.

Much more can be said about the qualities and functions of language in relation to culture, but that is not relevant to the purpose of this book. The purpose here is to establish the missing link between transpersonal psychology and spirituality, which can be viewed as one of the major factors of distortions instead of a bridge between the East and West, psychology and spirituality, and reason and passion.

The intention is not to claim superiority for the Sanskrit language. The only point to make here is that the Sanskrit language is most effective in creatively expressing human experience. Life is only truly lived in experience, not in thoughts and concepts. Psychotherapy is about helping to relate to one's experiences, thus making clients consciously aware of their reactions (past memories) to certain situations. Psychotherapy facilitates the transformation process of change at a certain level of consciousness. Can words ever express how one feels? However, when someone knows different languages, it is possible to know which language feels closer to expressing what has been experienced, although no language is able to interpret an experience fully.

When the word *akash*, therefore, is understood from a cultural and philosophical viewpoint, it connects to the meaning of its source. In this instance, the word *akash* has a Vedic philosophical meaning that integrates all human sciences.

As indicated in *Śiva Sūtras* (Singh 1979), the divine consciousness in its form as creative energy is known as *Kundalini*. She is the seed and life of all. From her is produced the group of three letters, namely: *anuttara* (indicating "a"), *icchā* (indicating "i"), and *unmesar* (indicating "u"). From this triad are produced the various letters. Each of these—*anuttara* ("highest reality"), *icchā* ("willpower"), and *unmesar* ("knowledge")—has five *shaktis* ("divine power") of: *cit* ("the consciousness that is the unchanging principle of all changes"), *ananda* ("bliss"), *icchā* ("willpower"), *jnaňa* ("intelligence"), and *kriya* ("activity"). From each of these arises a group of five letters, *vācaka* ("name indicator") and a corresponding group of five *tattvas* ("elements or aspects of reality") as *vācya* ("objects of these names"), viz, gross elements, *tanmatras* ("organs of action, organ of sense, and psychic apparatus").

The letter "a" of *akash* is the expression of *cit-sakti*, representing *anuttara*, the highest *shakti* ("power"). That is the origin of all letters. The Vedantic meaning of *akash* ("sky") will be the subtle and ethereal fluid filling and pervading the universe as a vehicle of life and of sound. The divine power source of "a" is also known as "I consciousness." So, when seeing *akash*, Meera's being fills with the experience of these qualities and she relates to a bigger picture.

The main idea here is to sample some of the power of these words, although there is much more that could be experienced. When philosophically understood, their power penetrates many layers of consciousness and enables people to have a deeper and insightful understanding of that word.

Meera says that depth is of the utmost importance, for it is this depth that enables her being to withstand the intensity of the currents of universal energies that she has opened herself up to in order to experience *akash*. She says, "When I look up at *akash* with *bhakti bhav* ('reverence'), which means ultimate emotional connection, I am also connecting with my true nature." She also points out, "Spirituality is eternal, whereas psychology is a mere human effort to understand it," and we must honour the difference.

Some people might argue that this misrepresents the breadth of Western thought. In fact, the central argument of this book is that, in the West, the abstraction of the features of this world leads to categorization of language into subject and object.

From the subjective view of a human being, there is a somewhat singular understanding of the world. For example, when Meera looks up, she identifies what she sees as *akash*, as opposed to the word "sky," which reflects her knowledge and experience derived from the Vedic texts. In Western language construction, however, "sky" is what people view if they glance up towards the region of the atmosphere and outer space as seen from the Earth; thus, for Westerners, the sky is the object of their subjective view, a concept that is again a thought process and limited by mind and reason (logic). As such, they experience "sky" outside themselves. They are not living it, so this immediately reduces their relationship with the sky, creates a separateness, distance, and an individuality. The difference indicated gives further rise to structure and boundaries, while the ego maintains doubts and fears about the sky.

In the West, therefore, human beings stand back from the sky to view a mental representation of their understanding. In the East, understanding is drawn from a meaning that incorporates the experience of *akash* ("sky") in a holistic sense that is a direct part of that experience, not once removed from the concept of sky. Thus, Meera's experience of *akash* allows her to be at one with it, not as a subject observing an object called "sky." Her awareness and knowledge of both languages, enables her to appreciate this significant difference.

This difference is an important feature that highlights the contrast between the "being" and "doing" of the Eastern and Western worlds, respectively, and how language can create a multi-levelled understanding of the world, which can be communicated more clearly to someone within one's own culture; whereas, between cultures, the meaning can be lost in the translation of understanding, being merely slotted into a view of the world coloured by preexisting mental representations. It is easy, therefore, to see how meaning can be misrepresented and misinterpreted.

Bringing this realization to the fore with an open mind can bring greater understanding, which can be best gained through experiential learning. Perhaps it is unreal and unjust to expect a Western mind, with a totally opposite philosophy and values system, to understand the meanings inherent in Eastern spiritual words.

In the view of L. S. Vygotsky (1988), the pattern of social interaction in different cultures determines the structure and pattern of internal cognition: the very mechanism underlying higher mental functions is a copy from social interaction; all high mental functions are internalized social relationships. Thus, if the culture has a radically different understanding of the world, and what being in the world means, it is not surprising that the minds of the people within different cultures will be constructed in such as a way that may prohibit understanding.

Swiss psychologist Jean Piaget (1896–1980), however, argued for what has been termed "constructivist theory," whereby human cognitive development goes through sequential stages that bring us to higher levels of thinking. If this is considered as a possibility, it may be that people in the Western world have become stuck at some lower level of understanding at a cognitive level because of what one might term constraints of the language, and that the eastern mind has moved to higher levels of consciousness, having the necessary meaning of words within the language.

Here, we will explore a few more Sanskrit words, where the translation has distorted the real meanings of the words.

In Chapter 1, for example, we mentioned that there is no word in Sanskrit for "spirituality," and in translation, it has been compromised by use of the word *adhyatmik* (study of the self or soul), and even the word *adhyatmik* is not translated properly.

The word *adhyanan* represents the meditative quality of the waking state of consciousness. The translation of the word as "study," therefore, immediately drastically reduces its meaning. The word *atmik* also cannot be confused with "soul," because soul is not *Atma*, and there is no translation for *Atma*; it can be experienced but not defined. The only way to understand it is by saying that "I am *Atma*," not "I have *Atma*" (the way people talk about the soul). If one can define or describe consciousness, then maybe one can understand *Atma*. The sentient or conscious principle can be known as *Atma*, or it can also be understood in a metaphoric language as like magnetism in a magnet, which is something other than a piece of iron.

Ordinarily, faith is fear; it is related to helplessness and insecurity. The oldest Buddhist writings (in Pali) use the word *shaddhā* for faith. The Sanskrit form of *shaddhā* is *śraddhā*, which is not accurately translated as "faith"; it means confidence, faith, in oneself.

The Sanskrit term *śraddhā* has a more comprehensive meaning than the English word faith; it means a sense of trust in one's higher self, in that which is more than body and which sustains the body. Accordingly, one can say that until this deeper faith is awakened in human beings, they will take the attitude of being the doer and will depend only upon their own human powers, which could fail them. The Vedantic Cosmic Principle believes in one cosmic power, which resides within humans, declaring "Thou art that" (Śankarācārya 1947). When people feel separation from that, and are conscious of nothing beyond physical existence, their powers are limited, and it would be wrong for a person to take the monistic standpoint and say, as Christ said, "I and my Father are one" (John 10:30). The word *śraddhā*, therefore, is not expressed holistically when translated into English as "faith."

The same is true for the word *srishti*, which expresses "the universe" (this word does not mean creation as it is understood by Western scholars). Again, translating it from Sanskrit to English is almost a hopeless task. Perhaps, the best that can be done is to explain *srishti* as projection. As understood within the culture of the language, *srishti* is the end of a cycle when everything becomes finer and finer, and it is finally resolved back into the primal state from which it arose. There it remains for a time in an undisturbed state (tranquillity), ready to come forth again. All these forces, as the pranas, resolve back into the primal prana, and this prana becomes almost motionless, though not entirely motionless, which is described in the Vedic Sūkta as "It vibrated without vibrations" – *ânidavâtam* (Vivekananda 2018).

There are also many technical phrases in the Upanishads that are difficult to understand. *Vâta*, for example, can sometimes mean "air," but at other times "motion." Not surprisingly, frequently readers may confuse them, which must be avoided (Vivekananda 2018). This is a part of the cosmological aspect with which translation fails to grapple, since it is not part of the body of Western language.

The English word "austerity" has a forbidding sound to it. The meaning of the word suggests mortification and discipline. Its Sanskrit equivalent, *tapas*, has a somewhat different frame of reference. According to Patanjali's *Yoga Sutras, tapas*, in its primary sense, means "that which generates heat or energy." *Tapasya* is the practice of conserving energy and directing it towards the goal of yoga and union with *Atma*. To achieve this, one has to exercise self-discipline and self-control.

According to Prabhavananda and Isherwood (1953), in the Vedic understanding of the word, true austerity is a process of "quiet and sane self-control," and as an image employed by the author of the Katha Upanishad explains: "When a man lacks discrimination and his mind is uncontrolled, his senses are unmanageable, like the restive horses of a charioteer. But when a man has discrimination and his mind is controlled, his senses, like the well-trained horses of a charioteer, lightly obey the rein."

In Western spirituality, austerity is generally regarded like a sacrament, one that can only be performed by ordained priests, and participation by ministers, at least among Catholics, is most important for salvation. As for Hindus, the act of ritual is simply a token of devotion and an aid to meditation that can be performed by any commoner without the need for a priest. The latter are valuable aids, but by no means indispensable. There are other paths available to devotees.

As we can see, during translation, the perceived meaning is what prevails, and the actual meaning of the word gets "mashed up," so that the end product is not the original picture, just an imitation. In everyday language, we use words like "ego," "intellect," and "mind" with meanings taken from the cultural language of the West. This creates disharmony between two languages and cultures; it is like remembering a name and forgetting the face. We will now examine a few more words where the English meaning of the word is not the same as in Sanskrit but is used in that context.

The Sanskrit word *ahamkāra* is translated into English as "ego." The English dictionary meaning of "ego" is "the part of the mind that mediates between the conscious and the unconscious and is responsible for reality testing and a sense of personal identity" (Oxford University Press 2010). Clearly, ego is associated with mind, brain and thinking, and in Western psychology plays an important role as "self."

On the other hand, in Sanskrit, *ahamkāra* (Singh 1979) means "I-ness." *Aham* is the personal pronoun "I." *Kar* means "make do"; hence, "I maker" or "I consciousness." In Sanskrit, ego is the component of the mind that claims sense impressions for itself and establishes them as individual knowledge. All doubts and decisions remain related to each other as long as they belong to a single individual. The constant concept of one's feelings, such as "I doubt" or "I decide," is a thought, and its functional name is *ahamkāra*. Vedic scripture proclaims that humans, in essence, are part of pure consciousness.

*Ahamkāra* plays an important role through its reflection in realization and development of the "Personal Essence." The presence of ego points to the reality of the Personal Essence, just as the existence of false gold indicates the existence of true gold. A. H. Almaas, in *Essence with the Elixir of Enlightenment: The Diamond Approach to Inner Realization* (1998), puts this clearly while exploring the term "essence" to distinguish the intrinsic core of human nature from its acquired attributes.

Similarly, the word "intellect" (which in the West is associated with the meaning of a condition of decision of thought) has a different meaning in Sanskrit. *Buddhi*, translated as "intellect," denotes a function of inner—the inner organs—which determines the true nature of an object. The word *buddhi* is derived from *budh*, which means to awaken, recover consciousness, hence the Buddha, the Enlightened One, the One Who Has Awakened. *Buddhi* is the power of forming and retaining conceptions and general notions; the faculty of mind that discerns, judges, comprehends; the discriminative faculty by which doubts are resolved and decisions are made. Discrimination, when it is real, rests on an illumination of the *buddhi*; this is the spiritual principle that, at the same time, is intelligence and will. It involves, then, quite naturally, a transformation not only of thought but also of human conduct. That is why, among the Great Beings who have "realized," we find such unity of thought and action.

The *buddhi*, like *manas* ("thought" or "mind"), is produced from the combined *sāttvic* parts of the five elements. (*Sattva* is one of three *gunas*, or "modes of existence," and is discussed later.) The five Vedic elements are: *bhūmi* ("earth"); *tejas* or *agni* ("fire"); *marut*, *vayu*, or *pavan* ("air" or "wind"); *ap* or *jala* ("water"); and *vyom* or *shunya* ("space" or "zero"), or *akash* ("aether" or "void"). There are two other functions of the inner organ, namely the *citta*, which seeks pleasurable objects, and *ahamkāra*, characterized by "I consciousness."

The intellect is the judging capacity, the discriminating and discerning faculty, that examines and judges the stimuli received by the mind, and communicates to the mind its decision on the type of responses to be executed (Śankarācārya 1947). The intellect can be compared to the banks of a river, which determine its direction and course. The intellect (*buddhi*), besides remaining in the realms known, can further penetrate into the "realms unknown" to investigate, contemplate, and comprehend new discoveries. The stabilized thoughts form a "willed judgement"; they are called the intellect (*buddhi*).

The Sanskrit word *manas*, usually understood by Westerners as "mind," denotes a function of the inner organs (*antahkarana*), which considers the pros and cons of a matter. It receives external experiences and transmits them to the self. Yoga provides only one term, *citta*, for this inner instrument, while the Samkhya school of Hindu philosophy studied the mind in three parts: intellect, ego, and lower mind. In terms of modern Western psychology, the lower mind, ego, and intellect are the conscious mind, and the mind stuff is the unconscious. It is produced from the combined *sāttvic* parts of the five rudimentary elements. The mind has a capacity to travel only to the "realms known." It is ever in a state of flux and is always the "doubting element."

Similarly, in Buddhism, the Sanskrit word *upādāna* is commonly translated today as "attachment," "clinging," or "grasping."

In *Letters to a Dead Friend about Zen*, Brad Warner reminds his readers that the term originally meant "fuel," with its usage extended later to mean anything that keeps a process going. Hence, it is "about our desire to keep things the same and the mental fuel that keeps that process going" (Warner 2019).

There are endless examples of words where language and culture play a huge role in changing the meanings of the words. A word cannot be simply translated from one language to another without distortion. It demands a great deal of openness to allow oneself to go into the depth of the culture of a "word." Maybe, one day, such understanding will be able to find expression in some form of new language, or create new magical words to form a bridge over existing distortions.

Today, with increased interest in the parallels between the new physics and spirituality, a new language is needed to investigate and understand the phenomenon of consciousness. For example, superposition, known as the "central mystery of quantum mechanics," is perhaps "ineffable." In *The New Physics and Cosmology: Dialogues with the Dalai Lama*, Zajonc writes that "language was developed on the basis of normal sense experience, and quantum phenomena go far beyond what we encounter in the macroscopic world of the senses. Therefore. . . . it would be forever impossible to reexpress the formal mathematical treatment of superposition in conventional language" (Zajonc 2004). Everyday language, therefore, has very clear limitations.

Chapter 3

# Distortions by the West

The illusion that cost India the efforts of thousands of years to unmask is the same illusion that the West has labored just as hard to maintain and strengthen.
—Herman Hesse (1877–1962), *Steppenwolf*

Ancient scripture says that existence consists of contradictions; it is vast enough to contain all contradictions, and it consists of polar opposites. They appear to be opposites to the logical mind, but in reality, deep down, they are complementary and exist together simultaneously.

While there are many examples of how Eastern traditions and practices are taken to the West, this chapter selects just a few of these (drawn from meditation, mindfulness, and yoga) and explores the distortions caused by the West to the Eastern spiritual practices, further discussing their outcomes and various associated concerns.

## Meditation in the West

In English, "meditation" has the flavour of "reflection." In English, there is no word that can be said to be the precise equivalent of *dhyāna* or Zen, so people have to use the word that comes closest: "meditation" (Prabhavananda and Isherwood 1953). In Japanese, *zazen* means "sitting meditation": *za* means "sitting," and Zen is merely a corruption of the Sanskrit word *dhyāna* (Warner 2019).

With the word "meditation," the question arises "On what?" because "meditation" in the English language means meditating *upon* something. For example, meditation may be defined as: "the act of giving your attention to only one thing, either as a religious activity or as a way of becoming calm and relaxed" (Cambridge University Press 2020).

Also, the words *dhyāna* or Zen simply mean emptying oneself of all thinking; it is not a question of meditating upon something. Meditation is without any effort. It is pure awareness, like watching, which is a natural capacity. A person does not have to do it, as effort will disturb the stillness and bring in the mind. No effort, no mind; it is a spontaneous awareness. According to Swami Ghanananda (d. 1969), former head of the Ramakrishna Vedanta Centre in England, meditation is a state of absolute silence, of profound peace, of not thinking at all, but just being aware (Monks of the Ramakrishna Order, 1972). Only in that awareness is it possible to see the truth. Certainly, there has been an ancient tradition in the West regarding the importance of self-examination. Marcus Aurelius (121–180 CE), for example, remarked that "those who do not observe the movements of their own minds must of necessity be unhappy" (Aurelius 2006).

It should also be understood that any idea that Asians find it easier to meditate, "while Westerners have more complex minds and therefore have a hard time meditating is racist nonsense" (Warner 2019), but perhaps it is not too surprising that, in the West, a few researchers have focused on unpleasant meditation experiences. In one study, 315 participants (25.6 percent of the survey sample) reported "particularly unpleasant" experiences (Schlosser et al. 2019). This was reported in a London newspaper (*Metro* 2019).

Nevertheless, meditation in the West has become big business. The meditation computer app Headspace, for example, is said to have annual revenues in excess of £82 million ($100 million) (Dodds 2019).

In English, meditation is often confused with concentration. In fact, concentration is only the beginning of meditation. Generally, when we say concentration, it is what we practise, which in Sanskrit is known as *upāsanā* (literally "worship," but also "sitting near" or "attend to"). The word *upāsaka* means the one who gathers mental energy and focuses on a particular object. The object of focus (the deity) is *upāsyam* ("worshipable object"). The effort to concentrate upon the *upāsyam* by narrowing down your area of concern and concentrating on a particular object is known as *upāsanā*. A stage comes where the *upāsaka* disappears and the *upāsyam* alone remains, meaning that the meditator completely merges with the object of meditation. In concentration, one is concentrating upon an object other than oneself and greater than oneself. Indeed, the object of concentration should be greater than oneself. Concentration on an object lower than oneself is not *upāsanā* but indulgence. Concentration is an aspect of meditation. In Tibetan it is known as *gom*, which means "to familiarize" (Dalai Lama 2001); that is, to familiarize oneself with the object of meditation time and again.

To understand its subtle nature, a comparison can be made with how a certain part of our brain works. According to Swami Bodhananda Saraswati (b. 1948), there are two sides of the brain, referred to as the left and right hemispheres, which should be balanced (Bodhananda 1995). The left side of the brain is considered the seat of reason, while the brain's right side is the seat of passion and involved with emotions, unstructured thoughts, and the unconscious. Reason might give us direction, but where there is no passion there is neither movement nor energy. When these two aspects (conscious and unconscious) are in harmony, it brings about fulfilment in life. In short, concentration is the capacity to put your heart and soul into the activity of the moment. "It is putting your mind behind your limbs. It is an activity of exclusion. You exclude everything and focus upon a chosen thing" (Sharma 2015b).

The next step is contemplation. It can also be called introspection and reflection. When the mind and the sense organs are totally absorbed in an object, it is concentration. Behind the object, however, are the sense organs; behind the sense organs is the mind; behind the mind there is something else continuously reflecting and illuminating all these activities. That is the *sakshi*, which means the "witness" of all such activities. According to Patanjali's *Yoga Sutras*, meditation is evolution in reverse; it is a process of devolution. Beginning at the surface of life, the meditating mind goes inward, seeking always the cause behind the appearance and then the cause behind the cause, until the innermost reality is finally reached.

Contemplation (Bodhananda 1995) means to remain cut off from the object and the mind that is interacting with the object. In the word "contemplation," *tem* means "to cut off" (from the Greek *temnein*, "to cut"). "Temple," therefore, means a place where one can be cut off from the world. In Indian temples, people's shoes are removed before entering, which means that by doing so, you remove your world also; you leave it outside and remain cut off from the world, because you are in communion with the God. Contemplation means to remain detached from the object and the mind that is interacting with the object.

Remaining in an attitude of witness-hood—*sakshi bhav*—is contemplation, which means you do not completely forget yourself or completely disappear into the act of concentration, but you know you have a higher depth. It means to remain identified with the light of consciousness, which illuminates the presence and the absence of the object, as well as the mind and its activities. It is the quality of standing apart from activity, yet remaining interested and engaged. You then have the depth of an ocean. Standing apart, in terms of understanding and continuing to do everything known as detached activity, is contemplation, detached concentration. It is the depth beyond the object and the mind. The quality of reflection and introspection is necessary. Real introspection is just allowing things to take place and happen without any interference or judgement. Non-judgemental witnessing of all happenings is contemplation, reflection, or introspection.

From concentration one evolves into contemplation—creating and leaving behind, a detached activity. It is in this state of detached concentration that true meditation is experienced. It is an experience of total collapse into the self.

According to *Vedānta* (Vivekananda 1955), *Jnāna* yoga ("the path of knowledge") is practised in two different ways: contemplation and meditation. In the classical texts of *Vedānta*, the proper method for practising contemplation and meditation is not described clearly; rather, it is directly taught by the teacher to the student. Contemplation and meditation are complementary practices. Without contemplation, meditation becomes a mental exercise; without meditation, contemplation becomes mere imagination. With the help of contemplation, a person comprehends reality intellectually, and with the help of meditation the reality within is experienced. Through contemplation one comes to *know*; through meditation one comes to *realize*. Contemplation is a prerequisite for meditation, for unless one knows intellectually that there are higher levels of reality beyond mundane phenomena, one will not begin the quest to experience those levels of reality.

The Vedantic method of contemplation is completely different from the Western method of contemplation (Tigunait 1983). In Vedantic contemplation, one reflects on the transitoriness, and hence ultimate invalidity, of the experiences of external objects and looks beyond the ever-changing phenomena of the world to search for that which is real. In contemplation, awareness of the highest goal of life, self-realization, is always maintained.

Questioning and analysis are the chief modes of Vedantic contemplation. One has to use rigorous logic and close reasoning to realize the truth of the subject of contemplation. Faith and dedication are then employed to accept the truth, and strong determination is brought to bear to bring that truth into practice in daily life. Reliance on religious and theological concepts of God, and on the practice of rituals, is discouraged in *Vedānta*. Religious contemplation is viewed by *Vedānta* as a set pattern of thinking based on mere belief.

The above description of meditation (Sharma 2015b) shows that the word "meditation," as used in the West, is not what *dhyāna* stands for in the East. It is made to look very shallow and has distorted the real meaning of *dhyāna* on many different levels.

If we go back to look at the difference of the meaning of words like austerity, ego, faith, and intellect, we can see that any misunderstandings contribute enormously towards distortions of such powerful esoteric words as meditation and yoga.

## Mindfulness in the West

Mindfulness, as Buddhist psychology, is the ability to know one's feelings without having to act upon them or be acted upon by them in an unconscious way. Mindfulness is perhaps one of the most essential aspects of Buddha's teaching. He taught that one must not escape into the concentration and absorption of mind to find tranquillity but, rather, contemplate on the "four foundations of mindfulness," in particular the body, feelings, mind, and the thoughts and emotions that he called "mental objects" or "mental factors."

Mindfulness means being aware of exactly what is happening in the mind and body as it is occurring, which further reveals how much of a flux people are in all the time. It is not what we are feeling that is important but, rather, how we relate to it that matters. The Buddha taught intensive mindfulness practice as a means of actually dissolving the perceived splits between mind and body, subject and object, and awareness and its objects. Once mindfulness is developed, there comes a point in the intensive cultivation of mindfulness when it proceeds effortlessly, when experience unfolds continuously with awareness, but without self-consciousness. Mindfulness is the most effective way of encouraging self-awareness, and is well recognized by many scholars and described as essential for human growth. As psychotherapy and meditation begin to come together, this function of mindfulness will prove to be pivotal.

Mindfulness practices are now common in the Western world. Elements of Eastern meditation techniques are emphasized, while the religious and cultural context of the approach is largely ignored. As such, mindfulness has been applied in alcohol and drug rehabilitation centres, hospitals, prisons, schools, centres for military veterans, and other establishments. It has been used to help treat addiction, anxiety, depression, rumination, stress, and worry, as well as to aid athletic performance, healthy aging, special needs children, and weight management (Wikipedia: Mindfulness 2019).

Despite mindfulness currently being the "hottest thing going" in the West, Right Mindfulness is just the eighth part of the Noble Eightfold Path of Buddhism. The tendency to cherry-pick from the East, therefore, is very much in evidence. Warner warns that people are currently "trying to secularize Buddhism by removing the mindfulness part and presenting it as a thing in and of itself" and points out that Buddhism is "a fully formed system of which mindfulness is just one part." This selective approach also applies to Vedic philosophy and practice. An argument could be made here about cultural appropriation, although there are "no more pure cultures than there are pure races" (Warner 2019).

## Yoga in the West

Yoga is another word that has become popular and gained widespread usage in the West, but it is totally misunderstood and abused without any hesitation. It is used commonly and loosely, and largely practised as if it were a form of physical exercise without any purposeful knowledge, depth, or understanding. It is very sad to observe this happening; it is like eating the peel and throwing the fruit away. A lack of meaningful understanding of language and culture could be one of the main reasons behind this.

Yoga is "an in-depth psychology that incorporates not only all human sciences relating to body and mind but also our soul and spiritual nature" (Sharma 2017b). Similarly, according to *Meditation: Monks of the Ramakrishna Order* (Monks of the Ramakrishna Order 1972), yoga is a science. It is applied psychology. Yoga is the most practical school of Indian philosophy.

The word "yoga" is derived from the Sanskrit root *yuj* (pronounced "yug"), which means "to join" or "to unite." It is the Sanskrit ancestor of the English word "yoke" (the wooden crosspiece that fastens over the necks of two animals and then to the plough or cart they are to pull together). Hence, it comes to mean a method of spiritual union. To achieve such union is to reach the state of perfect yoga. Christianity has a corresponding term, "the mystic union," which expresses a similar idea. Indeed, Christ's invitation is to "Take my yoke upon you, and learn of me; for I am meek and lowly in heart: and ye shall find rest unto your souls. For my yoke is easy, and my burden is light" (Matthew 11: 29–30).

The yoga system provides a methodology for expanding one's individual consciousness to universal consciousness. The various schools of yoga include Bhakti, Jnāna, Karma, and Kundalini. It is a deep and vast subject, so it is not possible or practical to discuss all of the various approaches to yoga here. Our focus, therefore, is on the most comprehensive approach, known as Patanjali's *Yoga Sutras*. Patanjali was the first sage to systematize the philosophy and practice of yoga. Various commentaries on this text have been written, of which Vyāsa's is the most ancient and profound. Bhoja, one of the classical commentators, defines Patanjali's use of the word yoga as "an effort to separate the Atman (the Reality) from the non-Atman (the apparent)" (Prabhavananda and Isherwood, 1953). A person who practises yoga is referred to as a yogi.

The yoga system is highly practical; it discusses the nature of mind, its modifications, impediments to growth, afflictions, and the method for attaining the highest goal of life: *kaivalya* ("absoluteness"). Since this method is described in eight steps, it is also known as Ashtanga yoga, the eightfold path.

As Prabhavananda and Isherwood note (1953), according to Patanjali, yoga is the control of the modifications of the mind. He realized that it is the mind that leads a person either to bondage or liberation; that most human problems are mental and that the only remedy to solve them is mental discipline. The mind is also the link between consciousness and the physical body. This is the reason that Patanjali places great emphasis on the study of the mind, and provides all the possible means to control its modifications and unfold its great power for higher attainment.

Theoretically, the yoga system is based on the same tenets as Samkhya philosophy and the teaching of *Vedānta* (Hiriyanna 1949). In Samkhya philosophy, the mind is categorized into three functions, or parts: lower mind, ego, and intellect, whereas, in *Vedānta* philosophy, the mind is divided into four parts: lower mind, ego, intellect, and "mind-stuff" or *chitta* ("the storehouse of memories"). In yoga, however, the mind is studied holistically, and the term *citta* is used to denote all the fluctuating and changing phenomena of the mind. According to yoga, the mind is like a vast lake, on the surface of which arise many different kinds of waves. Deep within the mind is always calm and tranquil, but thought patterns stir into activity and prevent the realization of one's own true nature.

As stated in Patanjali's *Yoga Sutras* (Prabhavananda and Isherwood 1953), these thought patterns are the waves appearing and disappearing on the surface of the lake of the mind. The more one is able to calm one's thought patterns, the more the inner state of the mind is unveiled. It is not difficult to calm the waves of thought patterns on the surface of the lake of the mind. It is, however, very difficult to calm those dysrhythmic and destructive waves of thought patterns that arise from the bottom. Memories are like timebombs buried in the lakebed of the mind that explode at certain times and disturb the entire lake.

There are two main sources for the thought waves arising: sense perception and memories (Prabhavananda and Isherwood 1953). Like lake water, when it is still and clear one can see deep down to the bottom of the lake. Similarly, when one's thought patterns are quietened, one's innermost hidden potentials are also uncovered. Since the mind is composed of the elements, or *gunas*, of *sattva* ("constructive," "goodness," "harmonious"), *rajas* ("active," "confused," "passionate") and *tamas* ("chaotic," "dark," "destructive"), the relative proportions of these qualities determine the different states of *citta*, the mind. It is the interaction of these three *gunas* that gives rise to thought patterns.

In yoga, the mind is described as having five stages, depending on the degree of its transparency (Tigunait 1983): "disturbed" (*ksipta*), "stupefied" (*mūdha*), "restless" (*viksipta*), "one-pointed" (*ekāgra*), and "well-controlled" (*niruddha*). The first three stages of mind are negative and act as impediments to the path of growth and exploration. At this level, one experiences pain and misery and all kinds of unpleasant emotions, but the next two stages are calmer and peaceful.

All the modifications are found in the earlier three stages. In the one-pointed (*ekāgra*) and well-controlled (*niruddha*) states, there are no modifications at all. In the one-pointed and well-controlled state of mind there is a predominance of *sattva*, the light aspect of *prakriti*. This is a tranquil state near to complete stillness, in which the real nature of things is revealed. This fourth state is conducive to concentration, and the aim of the yoga system is to develop or to maintain this state of mind for as long and as consistently as possible. In the well-controlled state of mind (*niruddha*), there is no disturbance at all, but a pure manifestation of *sattvic* energy. In this state, consciousness reflects its purity entirely in the mirror of mind, and one becomes capable of exploring one's true nature. Only the last two states of mind are positive and helpful for meditation, and many yogic practices are designed to help attain these states. When all the modifications have ceased and the state of stillness is acquired, then *purusha* ("consciousness") sees its real nature reflecting from the screen of the mind.

The yoga system (Monks of the Ramakrishna Order, 1972) categorized the modifications of mind into five classes: valid cognition, invalid cognition, verbal cognition, sleep, and memory. All thoughts, emotions, and mental behaviours fall into one of these five categories, which are further divided into two major types: those that cause "afflictions" (*klesha*) and "those that do not cause afflictions" (*aklesha*). Valid cognitions and memories are not considered to be causes of affliction and are not harmful for meditation.

The sources of valid cognition (Tigunait 1983) are perception, inference, and authoritative testimony. False cognition is "ignorance" (*avidya*). Ignorance is an aspect of consciousness, a certain way of knowing and bearing in mind the contrast that opposes the penetrating view of primordial intelligence to the ignorant mind. Ignorance is mistaking the non-eternal for the eternal, the impure for the pure, misery for happiness, and the non-self for the self. It is the modification of mind that is the mother of the *klesha*, or affliction. Ignorance has a further four offshoots, known as: I-am-ness, attachment, hatred/aversion, and fear of death (the urge of self-preservation).

Verbal cognition is the attempt to grasp something that actually does not exist but is one's own projection. Fantasies like *Alice's Adventures in Wonderland* (Carroll 1865) are mere verbal cognitions that do not correspond to the fact and only cause the mind to fluctuate, whereas sleep is a modification of mind in which one's relationship with the external world is cut off. But the dreaming and waking states are not accepted as modifications, since the dreaming state is occupied with verbal cognitions and the waking state is occupied mainly with valid cognitions and invalid cognitions. Memory, the fifth and final mental modification, is the recall of impressions stored in the mind.

The modifications of the mind (Tigunait 1983) are caused by impediments, namely sickness, incompetence, doubt, delusion, and confusion. These impediments disturb the mind and produce sorrow, restlessness, and a dysrhythmic breathing pattern. Yoga provides a method for overcoming these problems and controlling the modifications of the mind.

Patanjali states that the mind and its modifications can be controlled through "practice" (*abhyăsa*) and "detachment" (*vairăgya*). Abhyăsa, or practice, means a particular type of effort or technique through which the mind maintains stillness. Perfection in practice is attained through sincerity and persistence. On the other hand, *vairăgya*, or detachment, here does not mean withdrawing from one's environment; rather, it means to have no expectations from external world objects. Detachment means to eliminate identification with nature and to understand oneself as pure self, as a self-illuminating conscious being.

Patanjali also describes another method of yoga, Kriyā yoga, which means "the yoga of purification" (Prabhavananda and Isherwood 1953). It is a threefold discipline, composed of the practice of austerity, study of scriptures, and surrender to God. Patanjali yoga is a highly scientific path and combines many different practices in a systematic way, through which it is possible to develop voluntary control over the body, desires, emotions, thoughts, and the subtle impressions that lie dormant in the unconscious mind.

The yoga system provides many different methods to accommodate people of varying capacities, including Bhakti, Hatha, Jñāna, Karma, Kundalini, and Mantra. According to Patanjali Yoga, the eightfold path (Ashtanga or Raja yoga) has the necessary qualities and conditions for reaching the subtler levels of consciousness, which eventually leads to realization of the highest state of consciousness.

The esoteric traditions of the East need to be taken seriously and require deep, meaningful understanding in order to get the desired results. Adopting a shallow view leads to distortions, as suggested earlier. It can be argued that distortion is also a two-way process; it not only devalues the ancient esoteric systems but also misguides and confuses the practitioner through misinformation, and one cannot be sure of getting the desired results. In some yoga and meditation classes in the West, people are not even given clear, proper instructions about sitting postures, what it means to be watchful of your breath (*prana*), and what the pros and cons are of these systems. Meditation and yoga systems demand intense training and discipline, and eventually this leads to integration of being. This is the main purpose behind them: the total unfolding of human potential. In order to earn the necessary grace, one has to undergo spiritual discipline. This is known as yoga.

As noted, in the West (certainly in the United Kingdom), these systems are unfortunately frequently used as a method of doing something, such as going to the gym or practising aerobics; meditation is mostly confused with concentration; and yoga is confused with stress management and fitness exercises. In this regard, the East and West are different in many respects; they are the two opposite poles supporting the universe, but there is a unity in this diversity that is creative and positive. By revering this difference, it is possible to rejoice in the beauty it represents, instead of deforming it to suit the comfort of a materialistic lifestyle.

## Assumptions About Religions, Culture, and Tradition

The eight oldest religions in the world still extant are: Hinduism (founded around the 15th – 5th century BCE), Zoroastrianism (10th–5th century BCE), Judaism (9th–5th century BCE), Jainism (8th–2nd century BCE), Confucianism (6th–5th century BCE), Buddhism (6th – 5th century BCE), Taoism (6th–4th century BCE), and Shintoism (3rd century BCE–8th century CE) (Leser 2018). The major religions of the world, therefore, are of Asiatic origin.

Evidence from several sources has revealed that a close relationship between Hinduism and Christianity does exist (Satprakashananda 1975; Kersten 1994). There are many common features in the two religions. To start with, Christ and Krishna are worshipped as divine incarnations, whereas the founders of other religions are regarded as prophets or messengers of God. The climax in both religions is faith in the incarnation of God, and both declare that God incarnates Himself in human form.

Despite such similarities, it can be argued that Hinduism is not properly understood in the West. There are many incorrect assumptions and misconceptions about it. Hinduism (Vedic tradition) is often confused with Buddhism, and Eastern wisdom is frequently talked about in reference to Buddhism, whereas Eastern wisdom is not contained in Buddhism but Buddhism is contained in Eastern wisdom. Actually, Buddhism does not accept the authority of the Vedas, although the importance of direct experience (self-realization) is maintained even in Buddhism, together with many views held in the Vedas. Buddha, however, did not cite the Vedas as the authority for his views.

In Vedic traditions, religion is understood as the science of self-purification; it is a means to an end. The Sanskrit word for "religion" is *dharma*; it also means "duty," that is, the duty towards oneself to realize one's full potential. The word religion, therefore, represents the meaning of any technique by which people regain their original glory (Tigunait 1983). In fact, the merger of the "little self" (ego) with the "real Self" (*Atma*) is the goal of religion. Hinduism as a religion represents a way of life. Contrary to the view of many Westerners, it is free from rituals and superstitions, and is meant to bridge the gulf between people and God.

Similarly, Eastern cultural traditions are rich and include, for example, sexuality, an important part of Eastern culture and religion. In India, men and women dress very differently from each other. Dress is different in every sense—colour, cut, stitching, even the material used—unlike in the West, where we find both men and women wearing trousers. In the East, femininity is honoured and admired, and allowed to express itself in every sense— dress, jewellery, hairstyles, even the toiletries and make-up used by women. But everything has a deep spiritual meaning behind it.

For example, the mark Indian women wear on their forehead between the eyebrows (known as *bindi*) denotes feminine wisdom, the quality of the sixth chakra (energy centre) of Kundalini yoga. Similarly, the bangles Indian women wear symbolize their retaining of feminine tenderness, that those nurturing and caring arms should stay away from the hardness of masculine tasks.

Henna is used for colourful decoration of young women, especially when they are courting or getting married. This has a deep spiritual meaning, associated with the universal principle of feminine and masculine creativity. A young woman's body adorned with the colour of henna (*mehandi*) denotes *prakriti* (the "feminine" or "anima") manifesting herself out of compassion for *purusha* (the "masculine" or "animus"). The purpose of the manifestation of *prakriti* (feminine) is to show herself to *purusha* (masculine), so that he can realize that he is distinct from her. It is a living example of Vedic people living a cosmic life, a universal principle expressing itself in its simplest form in everyday life as man and woman.

These are only a few examples of the richness of culture and tradition in the East. One could cite many more examples, but the point is that these traditions have lost their value and richness in the West—people use them as fashion or as part of their make-up. It can be argued that these traditions had a special effect on people when they were followed with that kind of deep understanding of their meaning; now they are there like a worthless piece of plastic. These traditions are assumed to be from a Third-World country, apparently, and not considered worth exploring in their deeper sense, which again could reveal their true meaning in the way it was experienced by ancient practitioners. People in the West appear to be quite precise and more interested in action than motivation, whereas, in the East, motivation is more important than action; indeed, it is hard to judge the value of an act without precisely referring to what lies behind it. The energy of life or human activity is believed to be in intention. This is a sad situation, which creates a bigger gulf between the East and West instead of bridging it.

# Chapter 4

# Implications for Psychotherapy

The spiritual development of the West has been along entirely different lines from that of the East and has therefore produced conditions which are the most unfavourable soil one can think of for the application of yoga.
—C. G. Jung (1875–1961),
*Yoga and the West*

In the previous chapter, areas of distortions were explored and perceived disadvantages were discussed. To some extent, this observation reveals the expressive uniqueness of thoughts of each tradition and related uniqueness of each particular language. This chapter explores its implications for psychotherapy, and associated possible advantages and disadvantages, which may lead into an interesting landscape of ideas.

## *The Relationship Between Yoga Psychology and Western Psychology*

All knowledge is based on experience; this is the major common factor, both in yoga and psychotherapy. Therapists do not hand over advice or solutions to their clients; rather, they explore their emotions to help them be in contact with their experiences, which perhaps they have suppressed for a long time. The teachers of the science of yoga declare that religion is not only based upon the experience of ancient times but that nobody can be religious until they have the same perceptions themselves. Yoga is the science that teaches people how to get these perceptions.

About 900 BCE, or perhaps earlier, Patanjali crystallized some of these teachings. His Eightfold Path is the basis of Ashtanga or Raja yoga, whereas the Vedas and Upanishads were direct cognitions of the mechanics and structure of the universe, which came to *rishis* ("seers") in a higher state of consciousness. In experiencing this inner knowledge, sound was of great importance. "Vibration of sound" (*śruti*) evoked such energies and physically prepared people to the level necessary to withstand the powerful experience of the spirit's integration with matter. Sacred geometry, through the use of *mandalas*, or the geometric configuration of symbols representing the cosmos, was the most powerful tool in understanding one's own inner nature.

The word *mandala* is rooted in Sanskrit and means "circle," which is the first enclosed archetype of sacred geometry. The single point at the centre of the circle is called the *bindu*. The construction and meditation of spiritual mandalas is an important aspect of Buddhism and Hinduism. Mandalas are to be found all over the Orient and are used as a tool to facilitate contemplation and meditation. This process of experiencing mandalas has the potential of moving the witness into their spiritual centre. The contemplation of sacred geometry through the processes of studying or creating mandalas (open-eyed meditation) can lead the student to enlightenment. The circle is the first two-dimensional archetype, a metaphysical doorway to God, Mind, and Oneness. No doubt, Jung was captivated by mandalas, not merely because of his attraction to Eastern philosophy but also because he saw the circular images as representing the self or totality of the personality. Barry Jeromson (2005–2006) states that Jung illustrated his first-known mandala-inspired work, *Systema munditotius* ("The System of All Worlds"), in 1916.

Another development in this area was *Vedānta*, whose chief exponent, Adi Shankaracharya (788–820 CE), brought to light its creative evolutionary aspect. In the 19th century, there was a renaissance in yoga. The key figures in this movement were Rabindranath Tagore (1861–1941), Mahatma Gandhi (1869–1948), Swami Vivekananda (1863–1902), Sri Aurobindo (1872–1950), Tirumalai Krishnamacharya (1888–1989, often called "the father of modern yoga"), and others. The idea of this movement was to improve society, which was globally going downhill. The emphasis was on the idea of the creative evolutionary aspect of the self in relation to society.

In conclusion, it can be said that during this time in the West, Sigmund Freud (1856–1939), Alfred Adler (1870–1937), and Carl Gustav Jung (1875–1961) were trying to make sense of what life is about, what the role of mind is in creating people's realities and delusions, and what is the self, and how is it different and unique from one person to another? It appears to be very analytical and all very ego-based and external, separate from one's inner experiences. Before the 20th century, mental illness was perceived as a separation from society as well as a person's true nature. Patients, therefore, were thought to be alienated both from society and their true natures, hence were insane. As such, someone who studied the pathology of mental illness was originally referred to as an "alienist" (Carr 2018) rather than a "psychiatrist," a term that was first used around 1869 (Merriam-Webster 2020).

For a long time, it appears that women were not given much consideration in Western psychology; the feminine aspect of human nature was overlooked and ignored. It was only comparatively recently that the idea of the rejected feminine was introduced by Jung. Before that, Western psychology remained under the construct of masculine nature only, missing out on the feminine qualities of creativity, insightfulness, intuition, openness, receptivity, and the ever-changing feminine aspect, both rational and irrational. In Eastern traditions, however, this aspect of feminine and masculine seemed to be well integrated, thus less threatening for people to go inward and experience themselves as a whole.

According to old scripture, duality is an important step on the ladder to self-realization, but where it stops is not the ending. According to Tigunait (1983), "non-dualism" (*advait*) reality is beyond materialism, causation, number, and structure. This same conviction is expressed in the philosophy of *Nirguna Brahman* in *Vedānta*, in the concept of *shunyata* in Buddhism, in the concept of *tao* in Chinese philosophy, and in the philosophy of *tattvatita* in Tantra. In contrast to Tantra, *Vedānta* stresses the method of self-inquiry. Sri Aurobindo's Integral yoga philosophy, therefore, lies in the active and effective awareness of the individual with the superconscious Divine.

It would appear to be consistent with previously reported findings to speculate that in Eastern philosophy the goal of life is to realize the infinite, the absolute, or Self. The emphasis is on direct experience, rather than an intellectual understanding. As the word *Brahma* comes from the root *bri*, which means "to grow or expand the Ground of Being," this also points towards our unlimited potential. That is to say that our own essential nature is unmanifest *Brahma*. There lies within us the possibility of experiencing it, which is consciousness itself. As this consciousness vibrates, it becomes the substance of our own thoughts and experiences. Pure consciousness is the Self (*Atma*); it is not the personality, ego, or the contents of the mind, just as a beam of light is not the object it illuminates. In transpersonal psychotherapy, the therapist is that beam of light, like the sun that is available with its vitality and qualities, not imposing or enforcing them, but trusting that clients will take whatever is needed to unfold their potential, like a sunflower unfolds in the presence of the sun.

As Vedantic philosophy reveals, there is an interplay between *prakriti* ("anima") and *purusha* ("animus"). *Prakriti* is the primordial potential for matter, unconscious creative energy, whereas *purusha* is spirit, consciousness (Tigunait 1983). The creative energy of nature is manifested in humans as psychic energy (*chitta*). Whatever nature does is for the "enjoyment," or *bhoga*, of liberation of spirit. *Bhoga* also means participation in the dualities of existence.

In that sense, it seems that when Freud talked about the "pleasure principle," he was limiting himself to the animus part of it, making the relationship with the mind's manipulative nature, and did not fully participate in the duality as a means of perceiving the bigger picture where, through union, liberation from suffering is possible. Even Jung, who mastered the feminine and masculine (anima/animus) principle of human nature, could not allow himself to go beyond archetypes of the contra-sexual.

Although there appear to be some interesting and noticeable points of similarities and differences between Western psychology and yoga psychology, it would be unfair to compare them, since yoga psychology can be regarded as a finished product, whereas Western psychology is still developing and continually changing.

Perhaps because of this difference, Western therapists who do not recognize the existence of the *Atma* ("the Godhead within") are unable to help their clients achieve the union of perfect yoga. It seems that they stay with their own sense of security, beyond which they cannot allow themselves to venture. Even though they may recognize the possibility and outstanding advantage of such spiritual integration, due to their own fears they prefer not to make it a part of their therapy. The two, therefore, are kept separate.

## Pathology and Spirituality

It would appear to be consistent with the previous discussion to speculate that identification with affective experience may provide people with the most consistent sense of self. In the first few years of a child's life, affect perception and cognition are intimately woven together. J. Daniel Brown notes in *Masks of Mystery: Explorations in Christian Faith and the Arts* (1997) that, as adults, affect and cognition may continue to be fused, and the task of psychotherapy is thus to assist clients in clarifying the affective elements from situations and relationships that give rise to them.

As we have seen in spiritual development, one's relationship with affect may change profoundly. A person may encounter earth-shattering qualities of emotion, and also disassociate and modify many habitual emotional patterns. Intuitive knowledge, which is experiential and direct, is developed over time through sensitivity towards subtle and affective inner experiences. At the same time, in the field of mental health, affect is mostly perceived as negative, inappropriate, or incongruent. Some profound affective experiences can register at an unconscious level, expressed in symbols and metaphors and not experienced physically. These can be disturbing, in the sense that they reach the unconscious depths before touching the surface.

In the West, people who are experiencing psychotic episodes can find it hard to interpret these inner experiences and, therefore, their mood and feelings may remain unidentified or misunderstood. Affect is usually physically demonstrated (what may be known as madness) but not connected with feeling emotions.

Such people may have to associate with an object outside of themselves, for example, "I am really the Queen Mother" or "The radio is controlling my thoughts." They remain unable to identify with a common reality within, where they derive what is normally expected of those who are sane. In the East, though, this behaviour is normally accepted as part of an individual's expression without being labelled "psychotic." In *The Hidden Dimension*, Edward T. Hall states that a person's feeling "about being properly oriented in space runs deep. Such knowledge is ultimately linked to survival and sanity. To be disoriented in space is to be psychotic" (1990).

It has long been known that in different cultures and societies affective experiences are perceived and expressed in different ways, as many cultures in the world recognize the affective experience of "soul loss" rather than depression (Shweder 1985). Language is also greatly responsible for shaping exposure to people's feelings. The richer a language, the more one is able to express oneself. Often it is hard for someone to name a spiritual experience because it seems to contain all sensory modalities, as well as being affectively and significantly infused. Both profound ecstasy and anguish can be perceived as "not normal."

While pathologizing such human experiences, the role of culture, language, and religion is widely ignored or overlooked. For example, in Norway, the Saami, who are culturally greatly associated with snow, and have many words or names for snow and ice conditions in their language, can easily identify many different types of snow (Magga 2006). On the other hand, an American belonging to a capitalist and materialistic society could probably identify dozens of types of ice creams. There is a subtle difference in both states. One is to do with the nature of ice beyond form, and another is ignoring nature and focusing on the form only. Of course, you "can name things. It's just that the name is never a full description" (Warner 2019) because the actual experience always trumps words, which are merely symbols.

Sometimes, a culture allows these psychic energies to emerge and express themselves, so that illness can be avoided. For example, in their 2010 book *Spirit Possession and Trance: New Interdisciplinary Perspectives*, Bettina E. Schmidt and Lucy Huskinson describe the Saar/Zar ceremony in Sudan and Somalia, where women begin to behave strangely and talk in a different voice. They are seen as possessed by a spirit, and the male member of the family needs to pay for a special ceremony, including all the things desired by the affected female. This allows the woman to behave in a manner she is not normally allowed by society: dancing, smoking, making sexual advances, and so on. This experience is not looked on as any kind of illness. It is accepted and respected as a spiritual expression of oneself, yet it takes care of repressed emotions, physical and psychological needs, and arguably promotes a reduction in stress levels. In comparison with this socially integrated behaviour, people in the West might categorise it as "mental illness," showing that such categorization is very much a social construction.

In *Paths Beyond Ego: The Transpersonal Vision* (1993), Roger Walsh and Frances Vaughan compare altered states of consciousness—Buddhist meditational states, schizophrenic states, shamanic journey experiences, and yogic meditational states—and conclude that they are very different. It can be argued that there is a need for transpersonal psychology, more than ever, in order to broaden society's acceptance of the potential for such experiences to lead to discovery and personal growth.

## Philosophy

The comparison that has been undertaken is not intended to renew the problem as such, but to contribute towards the understanding of the effect of some differences (cultural, linguistic, and spiritual) on the development of transpersonal psychology. This chapter, therefore, compares and comments on different approaches against the validity of scripture.

These differences, which may initially be experienced as barriers, later raised challenges for Meera and motivated her towards finding the causes for such barriers and the possibility of reducing gaps in communication.

It is a very hard challenge to be authentic with others who have widely divergent value systems from oneself. It seems that people from Eastern cultures often compromise by suppressing their cultural and spiritual needs. By doing so, they not only devalue themselves but also deprive the Western world of an opportunity to learn about Eastern mystical and spiritual traditions. One can say that creativity requires risk-taking. When one has a strong sense of self, there is no fear of rejection, for how can people reject me when my existence is not dependent upon their approval or disapproval?

Ordinarily, society is divided into two categories: "heads" and "hands." The labourers are "the hands" and the bosses are "the heads"; the heads rule and dominate the hands. There is no third category—"the hearts"—but mastery and authenticity belong to this third group.

In the course of this book, a point raised is about love and compassion not having a place in traditional Western psychology. Indeed, humankind seems to have lost the language of love and compassion. Love is confused with being polite, nice, approving, and being totally inauthentic, whereas its nature is the complete opposite: love is being true to oneself and others, believing in directness, honesty, and equality—"Love rejoiceth in the truth" (1 Corinthians 13:6).

This is one of the many ways of defining love. It appears that people are more likely to be accepted in society if they speak the same language, whereas love is beyond language. It is, in fact, wordless. As such, when people stand up and speak the truth—the source of love—and create their own communication, they are not going to be liked, because they are causing a disturbance, shattering illusions, giving a shock to preconceived ideas and prejudices. So, for example, Jesus said: "To this end was I born, and for this cause came I into the world, that I should bear witness unto the truth. Every one that is of the truth heareth my voice" (John 18:37). His voice and vision were of love, but it still led to death by crucifixion. A person becomes a danger to the very foundation of the West, which rests on logical and rational discourse. It destroys their consolations and their rationalizations.

Perhaps confronting this fear is a fearful task in itself. Maybe, however, for the West to meet the East and a bridge of universal unity to be built, it is necessary to confront such fears of culture, language, and spiritual differences. Western narrowness and superiority need to be challenged, and the East has to provide a mirror for the West to scrutinize itself and conduct a painful self-examination and criticism. The Western ideal of external progress could be married to the Eastern mystics' desire for withdrawal into the soul. People could then rightly appreciate the rich possibilities of a full life and live in harmony.

According to Christian faith, God is perceived at a distance, thus ego is separated and independent from the unconscious. This narrow ego, which is identified with separate individuals, can create immense anxiety when any Westerner starts any kind of intensive meditation practice. Maybe their ego structure is not capable of handling the severe discipline that these practices require. In *Awakening the Heart* (1985), John Welwood puts this very clearly:

> For one thing, Westerners do not have the depth of resource that other cultures have provided their spiritual seekers. In India, the practitioners are coming out of a culture steeped in the understanding of rebirth and karma. There is a social system to support their practice. All of this is so deep in their beings from the beginning that they have a greater understanding of what spiritual practice requires than we do.

Welwood appears to be suggesting that the Western spiritual movement asserts itself into psychological systems that keep the ego strong; moreover, by associating it with enlightenment (the realization of the nature of oneself and reality), they cause further distortion to Eastern traditions. He also suggests that for the masses to benefit from Eastern spirituality, instead of the occasional few who are willing to go beyond their cultural restraints, new metaphors have to be found that are more suitable for Western cultural needs. Welwood (1985) also talks about the danger of distortion while using psychological language and concepts in translating or interpreting Eastern spiritual experiences. Psychology and science play a great part in both Western culture and religion, hence they cannot be ignored, though with extra care and higher awareness, a middle path is possible as a bridge between East and West.

Concurrent with the above findings, it appears that spirituality runs as an undercurrent through culture, language, philosophy, psychology, and religion. The relationships between psychotherapy and Eastern spiritual practices, such as meditation and yoga, have been repeatedly questioned. It can be argued that the task of psychotherapy is to expand people's awareness of who they are by integrating the parts of themselves that they had so far disowned, a process called "re-membering" (making conscious and whole that which was forgotten and separate).

Psychotherapy has different levels and functions to it, depending on the goals and the understanding of the client and therapist. It is an effective way of solving life's problems and of developing a functional sense of self. It can also help people deepen feelings and their sense of their inner life. In some cases, it may even help people begin to break through the protective shell that surrounds the heart, thus enabling them to be more receptive and open to the world around them, and able to meet others more fully. In short, it is a process of sorting out confusion and self-integration, but not self-transcendence. Perhaps it enables one to expand one's "I" sense but not dissolve it.

A good example of the Western approach to counselling may be seen in the ascendancy of cognitive behavioural therapy (CBT), which fits well into the rational, scientific, medical model that holds sway. In addition, some mention should be made here about the rise of various therapeutic methods that take their inspiration from Eastern spiritual approaches, such as compassion-focused therapy, mindfulness-based stress reduction (MBSR), mindfulness-based cognitive therapy (MBCT), and so forth, giving rise to the term Buddhist-derived interventions (BDIs) (Shonin, Gordon, and Griffiths 2014). Again, in this area, the West looks to Buddhist psychology without dipping a toe into the ocean of Vedantic thought.

Spiritual practices, such as meditation, provide an opportunity for us to let confusion arise and be there, living it, witnessing it, being completely immersed in that moment in our totality, without any "I" fixation. Meditation helps us tap into a deeper, wider awareness, which takes us directly to the root of confusion and allows us to face our fears. It provides us with an opportunity to experience directly our fixed identities as a defence against the uncertainties surrounding our lives. For a meditator, anxiety is not considered to be a problem. By not trying to find release from the anxiety but, rather, letting it be and facing it mindfully, the meditator strengthens the "muscles." This strength allows us to ride our minds, or go beyond the fear-creating mind, which further helps us to accept life as it is, trusting the process of life.

The nature of Eastern and Western spirituality (as explored earlier) appears to be quite consistent with current psychotherapy practices. Separating both psychotherapy and spirituality can be beneficial, in the sense that it can help prevent dangers and distortions caused by differences and misunderstandings. In essence, however, both do co-exist and in-depth psychology does become spirituality.

Culture and language play a significant role in psychotherapy. For a long time, this aspect of psychotherapy was ignored and overlooked, but it is beginning to get attention and much research has been carried out in this area. Indeed, for example (when examining Hispanics in the US), language "has been identified as one of the major factors that determine successful therapeutic intervention" (Padilla and de Snyder 1985).

One can say that culture is about individual differences, although many people are uncomfortable with the reality of dealing with those who are different. While most therapists do not openly engage in discrimination and oppression, there is always an indirect way; for example, failing to acknowledge cultural differences and judging others negatively when they fail to conform to the standards of the dominant culture. As Beverly A. Greene notes in "Considerations in the Treatment of Black Patients by White Therapists" in *Psychotherapy* (1985), the reluctance to acknowledge cultural and racial differences is often due to the individual's fear of dealing with the meaning of difference, and possibly coming face to face with their own oppressive and racist attitudes.

Some people seem to feel that difference is not so important and more attention should be paid to sameness. It can be argued, however, that too much emphasis on sameness can be an excuse for not appreciating the difference. While there are similarities between people, there are also wide-ranging differences, such as culture, ethnicity, gender, physical disability, race, sexual orientation, and social class. Differences make people interesting, and they can be very enriching if only they are allowed to flourish. According to Khizar Humayun Ansari and June Jackson, in *Managing Cultural Diversity at Work* (1995), counselling demands a diverse approach, which means valuing differences and treating people in ways that bring out the best in them.

Counselling and psychotherapy have their own norms and values. In other words, they have their own culture. One can say that each theoretical orientation in counselling and psychotherapy sets up its own culture. So, there is a cognitive-behavioural culture, a psychodynamic culture, and so on. It is possible that the person who is subscribing to a particular culture could be very rejecting of others who are not of the same orientation. It is quite obvious in therapists' behaviour, in their response to colleagues who do not use the same theoretical language as they do, and whose approach to case conceptualization is different from their own. Sometimes this type of behaviour can lead other counsellors to question their own competence and to feel de-skilled.

In *Race and Culture in Psychiatry* (1988), Suman Fernando writes that therapists have to recognize the barriers to communication that may arise from cultural differences; for example, a therapist's personal prejudice, linguistic problems, lack of knowledge of the cultures from which clients come, and so on. Therapists are part of society and, as such, are not exempt from prejudicial attitudes towards difference that can be seen in the wider society. A prejudiced attitude can block listening and can rob a therapist of the patience that is needed to attend to someone, for example, with a different accent. The therapist might also lack the skills necessary to work with people of different cultures. Writing in *American Psychologist* in 1974, Maurice Korman considers it unethical to provide counselling for people whose culture we do not understand

and for whom we are not competent to provide a service. Sue et al., writing in *Handbook of Multicultural Counseling* (1995) go further, stating that culturally unaware counsellors would be engaging in harmful and unethical cultural oppression.

While living in a modern multicultural society, one needs to understand that other cultures cannot be overlooked. Perhaps it is not the difference but the fear of the unknown that gives rise to all these biases. One can say that the unknown is that which has not yet been experienced. It seems to be human nature to resist taking painful risks. For many, it seems far safer to sit and make assumptions in one's head about another person's culture, feelings, and thinking than actually to engage in the experience with that person. Falling in love may be a good example of the fear of losing one's ego and stripping oneself to the point of exposure and vulnerability. How one resists taking the risk by making all sorts of assumptions about the other!

It seems that bias is just another form of defence. When a difference becomes a division, there is always an element of fear involved, and fear, it can be argued, is just an absence of experience. This is the very reason that all esoteric methods of self-realization are highly experiential. In traditional Tantra yoga practices, practitioners have to sit on a dead body all night, in the midst of a dense forest or *shmashāna* ("cremation ground"), meditate on mantras and then drink blood from a freshly cremated human skull to overcome aversion and fear. (This information is not drawn from a book or written text, but it still happens in India, and members of Meera's family have been involved in such practices.)

The same kind of methods were used in ancient Egypt, where practitioners were forced to have the most fearful experiences—experiences they would not normally bring on themselves—so that when they had similar experiences, they would become stronger and less fearful. In Egyptian traditions, the Crocodile Initiation at Kom Ombo Temple is an example of such practices. This is well defined by Drunvalo Melchizedek (b. 1941) in *The Ancient Secret of the Flower of Life* (1994).

It appears that in ancient esoteric traditions, the word "holistic" holds a deeper meaning than is understood by current psychology.

To ancient thinkers, it did not mean just bringing one's mind, body, and spirit into balance; it meant bringing every cell of one's body (*mer-ka-ba* or "light, spirit, and body") into balance. Special emphasis was placed on balancing the masculine (*purusha*) and feminine (*prakriti*), so as to have no tension between these two aspects of being; any such imbalance was considered to be a block in terms of evolving. What the modern world of science is discovering today, therefore, ancient races knew long ago: in order to survive in the higher worlds, we must first overcome fear.

Psychotherapy can be more effective with deeper understanding of the masculine and feminine aspects of human nature. It can be argued that most disturbances are caused by tension between the masculine and feminine. Jung also tried to grapple with this aspect of psychology. Tantra yoga, Egyptian alchemy, and ancient Western occult traditions have used it as the basis of their spiritual growth process. Wilhelm Reich (1897–1957) developed so-called Reichian Therapy, based on a similar concept of bio-energy as a modified form of sex drive (libido), which is supposed to control the whole human organism.

It can be argued that when one individual suffers, then society also suffers, and when any society suffers, then all humanity suffers. Indeed, a mid-13th-century version of the Jewish Mishnah states: "Whoever destroys a single life is considered by Scripture to have destroyed the whole world, and whoever saves a single life is considered by Scripture to have saved the whole world" (Philogos 2016). It is only through accepting and respecting differences between people, however, that bridging the gap between others can be accomplished. Even this is only possible if people accept and respect themselves.

Some therapists belonging to the dominant culture are uncertain of their own cultural and racial identity. The reason for this uncertainty is that they have never had cause to look beyond the fact that they are part of the dominant culture. As suggested by Wayne Rowe et al. writing in *Handbook of Multicultural Counseling* (1995), white people may not experience a clear sense of racial identity in the same way as ethnic minority members of society do, because for whites the salient factor that they must come to terms with is not their own difference, but rather that others are different. These therapists need to be engaged in self-exploring activities to find their own cultural identity. Spending time in an environment where they are in the minority would be a useful way for such therapists to appreciate their difference, as well as to acknowledge their sameness to others. Intercultural mixing is one of the keys to dispelling myths about other cultures.

Normally, the element of trust between the client and the counsellor depends upon the degree to which both perceive themselves as similar and acceptable to each other. Cultural differences, therefore, could come in the way of establishing a therapeutic relationship between the client and the counsellor. In order to provide an effective service to the culturally different, it seems important for counsellors to have the necessary training in cultural diversity, as discussed by Anthony Marsella and Paul Pedersen in *Cross-Cultural Counseling and Psychotherapy* (1981). It may even be useful to work with traditional healers.

Cultural differences might also make communication difficult, even in situations where people speak the same language. In some cultures, English words are used differently from the ways in which they are used by an English person, where words can have a different meaning due to people's experience according to their culture, language, and philosophy.

As noted by Clemmont E. Vontress writing in *Counseling Across Cultures* (1981), if the counsellor is unaware of a client's usage of certain words or phrases, there could be a communication problem. For example, in the current vernacular, the word "bad" not only means the opposite of good but also "attractive" or "sexy" (Urban Dictionary n.d.). Sometimes counsellors continue a conversation with a client thinking that they understand what is being said, when in reality they do not. At other times, they may allow the client to continue speaking, even when they are unclear about what the person is saying. One of the reasons is that therapists may be afraid to admit that they do not understand, and eventually this leads to more confusion and distrust within the relationship.

In Meera's counselling practice, she has noticed that Asian culture clients very often struggle to find an appropriate word to express their true emotions and then end up using some words from their own language. They probably do this because they know she is from the same culture and knows their language. As such, the question is how would they express their "true" emotions if they were sitting with a white counsellor who had more anxiety about their client's cultural differences than the client had about being accepted by the counsellor?

In *Counselling the Culturally Different: Theory and Practice* (1990), authors Derald Wing Sue and David Sue write that the counsellor's worldview also has a huge impact on a therapeutic relationship. Counsellors who hold a worldview different from that of their clients and are unaware of the basis for this difference are most likely to impute negative traits to a client. For example, non-religious counsellors who have a tendency towards conceptualizing problems from a psychological perspective will encounter a block when working with religious clients who view their problems from a purely religious perspective.

## Expectations and Assumptions

Expectations of the counselling process may be different for both counsellor and client if they are coming from different cultures. For example, some cultural groups may prefer a family approach to their problems, rather than the individualistic approach that is favoured by many Western counsellors. According to Marsella, Tharp, and Ciborowski in *Perspectives on Cross-Cultural Psychology* (1979), if a client comes from a background where they relate to authority in an autocratic way, then the tendency will be for them to do so in the therapeutic relationship. They also expect the counsellor to be active, instructive, and assertive. A number of writers (Baekeland and Lundwall 1975; Fischer 1978) have indicated that clients tend to drop out of therapy when their expectations differ from those of their therapists.

It seems the assumptions made about others are often influenced by one's own culture and, most of the time, people are not even aware that they are making them (Marsella and Pedersen 1981). Moreover, the assumptions made tend to be negative. If someone behaves in a way that differs from one's cultural expectations, they are seen as odd. Counsellors need to be more aware of the assumptions they make about culturally different clients, as well as be able to confront their own biases when dealing with any culturally diverse group (Greene 1985). This is of prime importance while working with difference, as personal biases influence perception of normal and abnormal. Writing in *Psychological Medicine* (1981), Roland Littlewood and Maurice Lipsedge note that it is not unusual for a Black family to be branded as pathological by white counsellors, whose view of normality is restricted by their culture.

Clearly, counsellors need to see strengths in different cultures and not be so quick to pathologize. Maybe then fewer ethnic minority group members would be labelled with a psychiatric diagnosis. In many ethnic minority cultures, the extended family, flexibility in family roles, religion, and various social networks can be sources of strength that can be used to support the client. By pathologizing, therapists fail to recognize these strengths and, therefore, cannot use them appropriately. Clients engage better and disclose more when counsellors are culturally sensitive.

Some therapists find it uncomfortable to work with people who are culturally different, and as a result of their negative values—acquired growing up through the family, the media, and so on—pressurize clients who are different to conform to the norms of the dominant culture, which makes a working alliance difficult. On the other hand, if this difference is valued, and a diverse approach is adopted, it is possible to bring out the best in everyone.

In *Handbook of Multicultural Counseling* (1995), Ingrid Grieger and Joseph G. Ponterotto state, "Diversity challenges the counseling profession to continuous growth, fluidity, and evaluation; it defies stagnation." Furthermore, notes Pat Grant in *Clinical Counselling in Context: An Introduction* (1999), when working with diversity, "counsellors have the opportunity to extend their roles and to work in different ways." Working in different ways also means being creative and being able to give expression to dimensions other than just the psychological side. At the same time, to go beyond the conventional boundaries of the psychological structure of therapy can feel very unsafe and anxiety provoking, as does the spiritual dimension that can come into psychotherapy.

Deeper exploration can take people to the root cause of their fears, which all originate in limiting self-beliefs. When people consciously make growth choices and, despite various fears, are willing to experience the feared consequences, it seems that letting go is possible. In the process, all that is lost is attachment and control, and subsequently, one is able to overcome the anxiety state, which then can be replaced by a person's living energy. With this kind of experiential understanding, a therapist can help clients face their emotions more directly, and the way people relate to their emotions is central to psychotherapy.

A transpersonal therapist's work with clients involves a strong spiritual bond between them. This works on many different levels. Some subtle levels are hard to grapple with and remain in one's experience and cannot be verbalized. However, it is possible to explore how spirituality supports therapy in clinical practice. Ideally, it should be possible to feel these energies working and feel supported by them.

It is only possible to work with what is known. When any action is performed that is free from personal attachment or interest, and when it is offered as a pure act of love in the service of humankind, then a spiritual action is performed. As such, when a counsellor is with clients with knowingness, grace, honesty, and, above all, acceptance of them for who they are, love manifests through the therapist. A non-verbal but strong spiritual bond is established between client and counsellor. Depending upon the client's circumstances or degree of their disturbance, it sometimes takes time, but it happens, and therapy only starts when this trust occurs. By being oneself, the client can be who they are. Clients should not be disempowered by being rescued but, rather, empowered by being allowed to face up to their own truth.

Some "heady" clients are intellectual and disengaged from their emotions. Meera recounts:

> We shared a turbulent journey, and now it is so gratifying to hear them say that their heart speaks to them, and they wonder how they survived all those years without listening to that voice inside them that guides them all

the time. I call it "heart therapy," which is based on Sufi philosophy. I first read about it in Sara Paddison's *The Hidden Power of the Heart* (1998). While reading it, I realized that most of it I was already practising. I find deep heart listening to be an outstanding tool for therapy. It involves keeping our energies focused in the heart as we listen. This attunes us to the other person's heart, bringing a more sensitive, essence-based understanding of their frequencies and words. By tuning into the essential being of the person, it is then possible to transmit an element and feeling of confidence and energy, which goes with it and can stimulate and encourage within them not just the will to survive but the will to live at all the levels of which a human being is capable. It seems everyone wants to feel understood in the heart. When I feel understood, I understand more. It is not about becoming my client's guide, as normally perceived by therapists. Instead, it is about guiding them to find their inner guide.

It may be argued that love, compassion, acceptance, and respect are vital qualities for growth and healing. It seems that no amount of clinical training or theoretical study is going to help clients unless therapists experience these qualities for themselves. As American spiritual teacher and psychologist Ram Dass (born Richard Alpert, 1931–2019) says: "What one person has to offer to another is their own being, nothing more, nothing less" (Walsh and Vaughan 1993).

According to Roger Walsh and Frances Vaughan (1993), spiritual issues and problems normally arise in psychotherapy practice, and very few therapists are equipped to work with them. Consistent with present findings, it appears that Eastern methods of meditation and yoga are invaluable, in that respect, in deepening a therapist's own transpersonal exploration. As explained earlier, meditation and yoga demand very high and intense standards of discipline and training, which are essential for fostering transpersonal growth. It is only possible to help others transform when we have transformed within ourselves. As the Buddha says: "To straighten the crooked. You must first do a harder thing—straighten yourself" (Byrom 2012). By means of inner exploration, the healing capacity of presence is refined, which actually is the essence of therapeutic relationship.

It is at the heart level that it becomes possible to feel accepted and cared for by another and, in turn, to be able to care and accept someone else (Paddison 1998).

With any kind of communication, an exchange of energetic frequencies occurs. As one listens to one's own heart more deeply, heart intuition magnetizes energy from the source to our system. It is then the head's job to formulate this energy into words to give us more knowing. It seems that the deeper we listen, the deeper the meaning is gained. The maths (head) gets broken down in a geometric sequence (experiential) to give us a more complete understanding. Paddison (1998) says: "There's math that covers all the corners and the whole room—from the micro level that can isolate a piece of dust to the macro level that can stand back and see the whole."

Deep heart listening can reveal to us both of these perspectives. One can say that practising such deep heart listening for ourselves in our daily lives can help us to stay away from disturbing thoughts. In Meera's view it is a kind of meditation—one might call it "meditational psychotherapy," which means having no identification with insecure thoughts and feelings when they pop up.

An example of this would be when Meera received some feedback on her MA thesis from her supervisor, whom she admires and much respects, but she flinched inside, feeling judged and criticized. When she meditated, however, and dis-identified with her insecure thoughts and feelings by surrendering them to the heart, she got a clearer picture. Meera realised that honest communication can put people in a vulnerable situation. After getting above the personal level (self-identification), she found deep heart listening to personal critiques to be a positive challenge. As a result, Meera could hear the truth without cringing inside. It freed her to feel the sincerity of her supervisor and to know that it was okay. It was no longer necessary to go through all the mental processing to understand her reaction. Just by going directly to the heart and staying in the universal flow, one can easily reach a common-sense perspective, which allows deeper understanding to emerge.

Like Paddison (1998), Meera began to realize that feelings of insecurity emerged when she identified with the fears that formed in her head and, at the same time, when the deep heart listening she normally practised with respect to herself had come to a halt. At the same time, she always tries to listen to others as she would like to be heard. There are times when Meera does get interrupted, when she has strong feelings about an issue. During such times, Meera feels that she missed an important opportunity, because deep insights come to people only when they totally listen to others.

In order to activate head–heart understanding, it is also vital to listen to the head's concerns with an open heart, which means listening with compassion to hesitation, doubt, or fear. In meditation, people are mindful of their thoughts and feelings but not involved in them; similarly, in psychotherapy practice, one can learn not to allow mental interruption to surface in the form of assessments or opinions. By adopting an holistic approach—fully focusing on the other person's essence, words, and deeper meaning—therapists have more to offer clients. When people perceive that they are being heard at the deep level of essence, they seem to be able to connect with their hearts and frequently develop their own insights and solutions because of the deep love they have experienced (Paddison 1998).

Basically, it is love that heals. Listening to clients with sincerity—on all levels of feeling, frequency, and essence, and with total attention—allows them to feel really understood; it becomes meditative and helps them to release their own heart wisdom. It seems that on many different levels, beyond conventional psychology, skills, and techniques, what works with clients is not really the therapist's psychological background and therapeutic approach but a deeper respect and compassionate understanding of the meaning that the client takes from their experiences, as felt in their hearts and how their souls were touched. It is the spiritual aspect that is relational between two souls, an exclusive experience beyond words. That is why it cannot be taken out of the consulting room to share with anyone.

In short, it is very hard (if not impossible) to give expression to spiritual experiences. As writer and martial artist Geoff Thompson (b. 1960) says: "The true truth can never be articulated; it can only be experienced" (Thompson 2020). In daily life, as the subject gets subtler and subtler, language becomes less and less effective in conveying ideas. Perhaps the seen objects can be described vividly, but the felt emotions are more difficult to express. Likewise, at times, intellectual ideas and ideals become almost impossible to convey.

## Linking Psychotherapy and Spirituality

Meera's fascination with transpersonal psychology proved disappointing to some extent when she realized that Western authors have drawn their ideas from particular religious approaches. She contends that most people in the West understand spirituality from a religious perspective.

Religions certainly preach unconditional love but do not necessarily practise it. Jesus, for example, makes clear that love of God is the "first and great commandment," but the second is, "Thou shalt love thy neighbour as thyself" (Matthew 22: 36–39). Religious people seem to be too attached to their belief systems, and this attachment brings and masks insecurity.

This may well be the case with different psychological approaches to psychotherapy as well. Sometimes therapists become over-identified with their particular model or approach to psychology and find it hard to "walk their talk." With some professionals themselves living a conflicted life, it can be difficult to guide clients to live up to the therapist's convictions. This dilemma has become an epidemic in current psychotherapy culture. It would appear to be consistent with previously discussed findings that insecurity comes from attachment and lack of trust, and this fear of insecurity leads to "difference," which further creates feelings of isolation, exclusion, and separateness.

This must be the reason that all spiritual traditions of the world teach not to be so attached and to develop love. For example, Lao-tzu (c. 6th–4th century BCE) says in the *Tao Te Ching*, "She is detached from all things; that is why she is one with them" (Lao-tzu 2000). Love is the opposite of attachment but, unfortunately, traditional psychology fails to talk much about love. There may be an element of attachment to structure, boundaries, and differences within current psychology culture, which is perhaps primary to its existence in its present form. If one looks at the growing amount of modern research conducted in this area by writers such as Stanislav Grof and Ken Wilber, it is increasingly evident that ancient spiritual traditions have developed effective means of overcoming such barriers to human growth, mostly through self-reflection on the fundamental question: "Who am I?"

Just recognizing differences of culture, language, and religion from a spiritual perspective may enhance a therapist's feelings of inner security, which may, in turn, bring about dramatic changes in their perception. In this sense, when the fear of difference is acknowledged, attachment to structure is also relaxed, which can bring about a sense of being part of a bigger picture. This feeling of being a part of a collective unit can be very empowering.

It may be necessary to believe and trust in one's own potential of being "whole" personally before even hoping to be part of a "whole." A holistic approach is not about joining one, two, and three together; rather, it is about experiencing all of oneself by relating to one's essence. It is a spontaneous unfolding. It does not take the meaning from *what* clients are saying but being aware of *how* they are saying it. It can be understanding the language of clients beyond the expression of words, by making a connection to their specific cultures, belief systems, ethics, morals, and philosophies, which means relating to their "being" and not just at the level of personality.

As Peter D. Ouspensky (Pyotr Demianovich Ouspenskii, 1878–1947) describes in *The Fourth Way*, essence is something we are born with and personality (a person's reality) is developed over the years, taking into account many influences and manifesting as opinions, views, and words. Ouspensky states: "Although the two are always mixed in life. . . . personality changes very often with the change of conditions, but essence remains the same" (Ouspensky 1971). When a therapist is able to relate to a client at the level of essence, any potential changes to the client's personality then become more of a possibility.

By introducing Eastern spirituality into psychology, the idea is to gain a deeper understanding of human nature and improve quality of life, instead of counting on any number of approaches available. Linking language, culture, and current psychotherapy to these spiritual traditions helps bridge the gap between essence and personality, and one can learn to communicate at higher levels of frequencies without causing distortion to either language or culture.

In summary, transpersonal therapy is a method of expressing spirituality in psychological terms and language, along with meditation and prayers. It helps to dismantle the barriers that keep human beings from the divine. All therapy is ultimately a spiritual exercise, because in facing ourselves we increasingly have the possibility of coming to know the divine within. Ideally, all therapeutic work would contain both psychology and spirituality. In particular, there is an opportunity with transpersonal therapy to integrate all these aspects in a conscious way. In her clinical work, Meera has the advantage of drawing on her Eastern background for an understanding of the philosophy and cultural meaning of words and language, as described earlier. In addition, it is valuable to acknowledge the difference between Eastern and Western approaches, as it helps broaden the spectrum not only of psychotherapy but also the entire human race.

Each civilization (East and West) has its own characteristic modes and, in general, shows the influences of languages, culture, and spirituality in approved forms or argument. This comparison may be used to spotlight differences and look at ways of merging them to facilitate positive growth. Our hope with this book is to offer a small introduction to a vastly complex subject.

# Chapter 5

# Conclusion

> There are many in the world who are dying for a piece of bread, but there are many more dying for a little love. The poverty in the West is a different kind of poverty—it is not only a poverty of loneliness but also of spirituality. There's a hunger for love, as there is a hunger for God.
> —Mother Teresa (1910–1997),
> *A Simple Path*

An Eastern orientation to life is increasingly important in the West, as people realize that there is more to life than what can be found within Western philosophy. The pursuit of knowledge is intrinsic to human nature and may be what has brought East and West together, despite their geographical divisions and other differences.

The modern Western approach addresses problems from an objective, theoretical, and pluralistic standpoint, whereas, the ancient Eastern approach is more subjective, experiential, and holistic. The West looks outward to external data, while the East turns inward to internal experience. One method is based primarily on dialectics and discursive deductive speculation, while the other is based on introspection and direct intuitive insight. In the Western concept, a person is a body with a soul, whereas Eastern systems consider a person to be a soul with a body. As a result of this view, in the West, the dead body is often buried to preserve it as long as possible (with Christians believing in the eventual resurrection of the body by God's power), while in the East it is burned to release the soul as early as is feasible; however, as the West becomes increasingly interested in the subtle aspects of reality, the basic assumptions of both philosophies are becoming less divergent.

The Vedantic philosophy of all-pervading consciousness and modern Western science are now coming to similar conclusions.

Quantum field theory and the theory of relativity are pointing towards the essential unity of all things, so the disciplines of physics and metaphysics are also finding common ground. Perhaps, in exploring the wisdom of the Eastern worldview, the Western world is in search of an intellectually satisfying explanation of the nature of reality, as this transition from materialism to idealism is evident in modern art, culture, and literature.

Western psychology, too, seems to be actively engaged in the exploration of the nature of reality. To find solutions to the mental problems on deeper levels, new branches of psychology have emerged, such as transpersonal psychology, the psychology of consciousness, and parapsychology (which investigates subtleties of life beyond mind). To understand what truth is, Westerners are increasingly investigating Eastern approaches in addition to Western ones, but due to professional and monetary constraints, psychotherapy is unable to integrate such high levels of spiritual understanding. A psychotherapist without a deep philosophical understanding of the spiritual nature of Eastern culture and language can run the risk of confusing the two approaches. Eastern teachings assume that a person already has a healthy self-structure, but modern society's crumbling family structures and traditional and community systems are challenging such assumptions and they are under threat.

This book started out as an exploration of the differences between Eastern and Western traditions. To establish this, we briefly investigated what lies behind differences between Eastern and Western traditions, looking at culture, language, philosophy, and spirituality; examined the source of their origins, influences, and impacts on daily life; and discussed distortions and misunderstandings. It was important to us to bring these differences to the light and show their current position. The more we investigated, the more frustrations and limitations got in the way, and it became evident that a compromise will be needed if we are to create a bridge to a more harmonious universal culture.

Ken Wilber's idea of surface structures and deep structures is valuable here. Wilber writes that surface structures are cross-cultural, universal, and invariant. For example, the human body is everywhere similar, but what is done with it is different for different people. In *The Eye of Spirit: An Integral Vision for a World Gone Slightly Mad* (2001), Wilber notes that the body can be used to play a game of football or kept in a still posture to be used for meditation. People do not learn to have a body, but they learn to use the bodies given to them. As discussed before, culture defines language. It is difficult to learn about one without the help of another. Difference is only visible when an opposite is present.

Chapter 1 explains spiritual development in the East and West, and the emphasis is on exploring the fundamental differences between Eastern and Western spiritual approaches. This section investigates the introvert nature of the East and extrovert nature of the West, linking it to the inner reflectiveness of the East and the materialism of the West. It concludes that the Western world may be said not so much to be wrong in exploiting its material resources but that, in the process of doing so, forgets to explore its spiritual resources. Similarly, as the 13th Prime Minister of India (2004–2014), Manmohan Singh (b. 1932), said, "India happens to be a rich country inhabited by very poor people." In its self-reflective preoccupation, the East missed exploiting its material resources.

East and West both seem to have something of value to offer one another. If the Western ideal of external progress could be married to the Eastern desire for withdrawal into the soul, there would then be hope for a rich and full life in this universe. The majority of ancient scripture teachings inform humankind that the union between body and spirit is possible and, indeed, the ultimate salvation from conflict and suffering, so this offers hope that a bridge between East and West can be created.

Chapter 2 explores the origins of language and culture and investigates developmental stages of both. While we looked at language from many different aspects, the esoteric and Western linguistic understandings of language are of real importance here. Esoteric language refers to the language used to describe metaphysical reality and enables the seeker to experience transformative processes. Letters as metaphors of reality have no transcendental external meaning; their meaning is in the minds of those who have learnt them. The esoteric aspect of the scripture is of a secret nature, couched in mystical language and understood only by a few initiates who actually practise the teachings and attain the highest benefit from doing so. Alternatively, scriptures are communicated in some cultures through metaphorical stories, such as myths and legends. Through their esoteric or metaphysical aspects, scriptures convey meanings that cannot be expressed adequately by any other means. They are symbols that can express non-verbal experiences that can alter one's consciousness drastically.

Based on reported findings, we can conclude that the very basis of language is metaphorical and symbolic, as it represents objects and concepts while not being these objects and concepts themselves. In *Language and Linguistics: An Introduction to the Study of Language* (1969), J. F. Wallwork stresses the symbolic nature of language and clearly suggests that when we use our symbols differently, it gives rise to confusion.

Chapter 2 shows how the understanding of culture, philosophy, and symbols can change the meaning of words. One may wonder if the teachings in the old scriptures are the message the Buddha or Christ was trying to convey or whether it is just a compromise? For example, their understanding that language can convey so many different meanings at different levels, dependent on the recipient's ability to internalize. Meera often finds it difficult to express her thoughts and feelings in any language, but even when she manages to do so, they are not understood by others as she has experienced them. Culture has a deep impact on language.

Differences and similarities between Eastern and Western cultures have been discussed at great length in this book. Language is also an expression of culture, and visa-versa; they overlap and both play a most important and active role in the evolution of human development. Culture is socially transmitted and profoundly affects a person's ways of thinking about and seeing the world and understanding relationships among people, things, and events. It seems that one understands the meaning of language according to one's culture.

In the course of this book, several examples have been used to demonstrate this. For there to be a richer, more holistic understanding of Eastern language, culture, and philosophy, we need to acknowledge differences in language, culture, and philosophy, or there will be only a superficial understanding of what the East has to offer in terms of reflectiveness and depth. The lack of understanding of a particular language and culture could be one of the major reasons for getting translations of Eastern scriptures wrong.

The "supermarket attitude" of the West (in supermarkets people pick up packets of food just by reading the label: they have little idea how the food got to the shelf and what it is going to do to them) has to change for the possibility of a bridge between the East and West to take place. By the same token, for some Indian people to sit and hope that life will bring them what they deserve without any effort on their part denies their inner authority by couching it in terms of the Eastern wisdom called *karma*. This is truly an exceptional time in the history of humankind, which calls for exceptional changes to take place. Instead of dreaming, one can wake up to the reality of "universal culture."

Through exploring the changed meaning of Sanskrit words, we tried to establish how deeply rooted human beings are in their inherent culture and language, and how they relate to mother tongue, cognition, emotions, sensation changes, perception, and consciousness. This shift in consciousness changes the meaning and our understanding of perceived reality; the subtlety of this unique experience can only be realized not described. Meera comments:

> Perhaps it is that when I penetrate the depth of my own reality, which is my true nature, I am able to energize it, evoke the fire to bring light and warmth into my being. This is the most empowering internal experience, which does not take the outside world into consideration. It is so enriching that outside temptations are powerless; it is like when I have had a good, satisfying meal I can go past a posh restaurant without even glancing at what is being served there. In modern society, circumstances and pressures are such that I cannot always depend on home cooking. At times I need to get a takeaway meal or go to a restaurant to eat. That means I need to get back to the

surface from the depths from time to time to know what else is available to me.

Remaining in the depths for too long can also cause resistance to touching the surface. As demonstrated in previous chapters, Westerners have a resistance to going into Eastern Vedantic depths and try to satisfy themselves by alternative means, which do not actually serve the purpose of fulfilment of their need to realize their full potential. Similarly, the East, completely absorbed in its inner depths, has faced difficulties in developing its external potential, so, despite possessing great knowledge and wisdom, India still falls into the category of a Third-World country. There is, therefore, a need for balance. It may be hard to maintain the continuity of such balance, but once this optimum point is reached, perhaps people will have the confidence to retain it.

As seen in the chapter exploring meditation and yoga, a great amount has been lost by not going into the depth of these Eastern traditions. These practices are totally experiential, beyond the realms of mind. Fear of going into such a vast ocean of experience is understandable. It is like being thrown into the sea when one does not know how to swim. Maybe some swimming training and understanding of the depth of the ocean could reduce the fear and might result in a more relaxing experience. Even the ocean can be tamed to some extent so that it does not appear to be so frightening. Once the depth has been experienced and one has come back to the surface, a clearer picture of what lies below has been gained. The surface can be appreciated and the depths not feared any more.

In this sense, the East shows more depth and the West shows more closeness to the surface. It may be necessary for us to take risks and experiment in order to bridge Eastern and Western differences. It is certainly possible. We may not get what we want, but we certainly can have what we need.

Third-generation Asians in the United Kingdom have given birth to a new race: they call themselves British Asians. They have assumed a new identity and have given rise to a new culture, language, and philosophy. It is a privilege to be present in this powerfully historic moment and witness such originality. It is a living example of creativity coming out of chaos. But one can only welcome this creativity when able to acknowledge it fully and be consciously aware of its outcomes. It also suggests that changing the meaning of words could also alter the meaning of two different worlds and unify them. It may not be the desired colour of black and white—the result may end up a grey colour—but this is what all the chaos is about: unity (*Vasudhaiva kutumbakam*) – "The entire world constitutes but a family" (*Maha Upanishad*, n.d.).

In conclusion, humankind clearly still has a long way to go. Our suggestion for future development is to adopt the means to reduce these differences. Living in a multicultural society has not changed people much in their attitude towards each other. It is important to have an openness and acceptance of each other's cultural differences and to try to overcome this fear of difference and develop love, respect, and understanding for one another. These are the weapons that will prevail in the war of "universal unity." A spiritual awakening within humanity is of supreme importance in order to awaken people to their inner reality and enable them to trust themselves enough to be able to trust others.

In general, people do not seem to have yet learned how to respect each other fully, share, and work together. The world, and all the relationships one takes as given, are undergoing profound rethinking and reconstruction. Creativity, imagination, innovation, and vision are required. International partnerships and interactions may be the essential ingredients needed for creativity in problem-solving, which requires a willingness to frame questions instead of depending on conventional answers. It means an open mind, an open heart, and a readiness to seek fresh definitions, reconcile old opposites, and help draw new mental maps.

Ultimately, it is the honesty of introspection that will lead to compassion towards others' experiences. Compassion will lead humankind to a future where the pursuit of individual freedom is balanced with the need for common well-being, and the agenda of humankind includes empathy and respect for the entire spectrum of human difference.

During the process of writing this book, Meera became aware of her own anger and frustration towards Westerners' reductionist attitude, which denies the inner depths of Eastern philosophy by distortions and reducing it to surface stuff. She states:

> I suppose, dominated by my own cultural values and principles, I held a prejudice against such results. Awareness makes a huge difference. I realized that it is impossible to translate anything without distortion, and it is even harder when translation is from a different culture and language, as we think culturally. Maybe it is nature's way of maintaining human evolution and creativity in constant flux.
>
> I also felt limited in my investigation of Eastern texts due to lack of resources and information. There are plenty of books available on Eastern spirituality, but most of them are by Western writers and would not have served the purpose of this book.
>
> Towards the end, I became acutely aware that throughout this book more emphasis was placed on exploring Eastern texts than the Western meaning of the same content. I suppose I assumed that the readers would have some knowledge of these words or techniques (meditation and yoga) as understood in the West. I have taken more time to explain the Eastern approaches, therefore, based on my assumption that the reader will know less about the Eastern approach.
>
> Being an Asian, it is not natural for me to use the indefinite and definite articles, and during the process of writing this book, I repeatedly omitted these from my writing, so that my English co-author needed to try and correct this. An "a" or "the" can dramatically alter the meaning of a sentence, which is precisely the point I am trying to make in this book.

In hindsight, the entire process of research work has been quite fascinating in the way it has unfolded itself, from where it started to how it continued through unfamiliar paths. It started by looking at the East and the West as two opposite poles. It was interesting to note that the differences separating them had a unique relational quality, as with men in relation to women. In a way, they also complemented each other. As in any couple relationship, there was a lack of communication between both poles. The important factors in eliminating this gap of communication seemed to be language and culture. Most of all, however, the cause of this attraction towards union of both poles seemed to be spirituality (the running undercurrent).

Ben-Ami Scharfstein put this very clearly in *Philosophy East/Philosophy West* (1978): "India is superior in its careful introspectiveness and at least powerful in its linguistic analysis, dialectic, and logic. . . . and the West. . . . is superior in its balance between intellectual analysis and social reform and in its ability to assimilate the attitudes and results of exact science."

This book is based on comprehensive discussions on the linguistic, philosophical, and other difficulties that arise in a comparison of culturally different viewpoints of the educational, religious, and social contexts in which philosophy has developed. It also discusses the relation of the different philosophies to their respective religions and scriptures.

Reading books on transpersonal psychology by A. H. Almaas, Stanislav Grof, and Ken Wilber confirmed Meera's views about language and cultural gaps, and gave her insight into the possibility of bridging the gap (union) via the spirituality that runs between both opposites as an undercurrent and deemed to be the source of universal wisdom. This research led to an enquiry into sources of cultural, language, and spiritual traditions, and with this came the realization of how much there is to know and the serious gaps in understanding among different theorists.

Some readers may find parts of this book hard to swallow. Indians, however, tend to be direct in their use of language. It is cultural—Indians in India speak without affection; that is, they are blunt. They say what they mean, rather than being attached to how people will hear their words, perhaps knowing that "niceness" kills authenticity. They belong to a population of over 1.3 billion people (Central Intelligence Agency 2020), though among them, women (in general) are frequently considered to represent less than nothing. Giving and receiving is a way of being in India; it is not counted and measured. Life is not looked upon as a business transaction. Meera comments:

> In the West, I often find that people are very eager to return a favour to you, whereas it was not a favour for me in the first place; it was a gift to another soul without any conditions attached to it. When I am doing something on the soul level, it does not require any wrapping up; it is passed on openly and unconditionally, unlike in the West, where great effort is involved in wrapping up a gift and expecting an equal return.

This book started from the middle; that is, it unfolded to create a whole, rather than having a linear beginning or end. Meera says:

> It was not a conscious or rational thing to do, nor was it a matter of will. It was a process of psychic development that expressed itself. Intellectually, I wanted to fulfil any academic expectations, which are very structured and demanded methodology. On the other hand, my Eastern mind wanted to just unfold from a centre point, a natural process. Unfolding only happens from a centre point, a simultaneous growth on many different levels. In my view, there can be no doubt that the unconscious laws of my being, and the purpose of these laws, is the attainment of conscious life. It is expressed in Chinese terms as *tao* and in Vedic terms as *sunyam*, which is the centre of everything.

Western thought is linear and logical; Eastern thought comes from the centre and unfolds. The highest point of spirituality in the East is *sunyam*. That is how the whole process and approach towards this book has been. There was no idea of starting from a point with a view to arriving at another point; rather, the book unfolded itself.

Writing this book has been a great challenge and a great comfort. The challenge was to dare to write down what it is that the authors actually believe in and practise, rather than hide behind other people's findings or research. It is daring to try to give form to spirit, to dare to separate wave from ocean, and to dare to try and express that which is inexpressible. There is risk, too, as the material presented in this book may not meet the standards that others expect. That possibility is true, but there is also love of the ocean. . . . and love is stronger than death.

# References


Almaas, A. H. *Essence with the Elixir of Enlightenment: The Diamond Approach to Inner Realization.* Newburyport, MA: Red Wheel/Weiser, 1998, pp. 29–30.

Ansari, Khizar Humayun, and June Jackson. *Managing Cultural Diversity at Work.* London: Kogan Page, 1995, p. 11.

Aurelius, Marcus. *The Meditations of Marcus Aurelius.* Translated by George Long. Watkins Publishing, (1862) 2006, p. 26.

Baekeland, Frederick, and Lawrence Lundwall. "Dropping-out of Treatment: A Critical Review." *Psychological Bulletin* 82, no. 5 (1975): 738–783.

Bahm, Archie J. *Comparative Philosophy: Western, Indian, and Chinese Philosophies Compared.* Albuquerque, NM: World Books, 1977, p. 54.

Balasubramanian, R. *Primal Spirituality of the Vedas: Its Renewal and Renaissance.* Philadelphia, PA: Coronet Books, 1996, p. 129.

BBC. "Scots 'have 421 words' for snow." *BBC News* (September 23, 2015). bbc.com/news/uk-scotland-34323967

Belur Math. "Swami Vivekananda's Speeches at the Parliament of Religions, Chicago, 1893." 2019.
belurmath.org

Bloch, Bernard, and George L. Trager. *Outline of Linguistic Analysis.* Philadelphia, PA: Linguistic Society of America, 1942, p. 5.

Bodhananda, Swami. *Meditation: The Awakening of Inner Powers.* Delhi: Surya Print Process, 1995.

Brown, J. Daniel. *Masks of Mystery: Explorations in Christian Faith and the Arts.* Lanham, MD: University Press of America, 1997.

Brown, Roger W. "Language and Categories" [appendix]. In *A Study of Thinking,* edited by Jerome S. Bruner, Jacqueline J. Goodnow, and George A. Austin, 247–321. New York: Wiley, 1956.

Byrom, Thomas. *The Dhammapada: The Sayings of the Buddha.* New York: Vintage Books, (1976) 2012, p. 9.

Cambridge University Press. "Meditation." In *Cambridge Dictionary*. Cambridge: Cambridge University Press, 2020.
dictionary.cambridge.org

Capra, Fritjof. *The Tao of Physics: An Exploration of the Parallels between Modern Physics and Eastern Mysticism*. Berkeley, CA: Shambhala Publication, 1975.

Carlyle, Thomas. *Sartor Resartus: The Life and Opinions of Herr Teufelsdrockh*. London: Chapman & Hall, 1831, Book III. Chapter III. Symbols.

Carr, Caleb. *The Alienist*. London: Sphere, (1994) 2018, p. 8.

Carroll, Lewis. *Alice's Adventures in Wonderland*. New York: D. Appleton and Co, (1865) 1866.

____________. *Through the Looking Glass*. London: Penguin Classics, (1872) 1991.

Central Intelligence Agency. "South Asia: India." In *CIA World Factbook*. Washington, DC: Central Intelligence Agency. Last modified June 17, 2020.
cia.gov

Chandra, Suresh. *Encyclopaedia of Hindu Gods and Goddesses*. 2nd ed. Delhi: Sarup & Sons, (1998) 2001, p. 151.

Chaudhuri, Nirad C. *Hinduism: A Religion to Live By*. Oxford: Oxford University Press, (1962) 1979, p. 312.

*Collins Online English Dictionary*. "Spirituality." 2020.
collinsdictionary.com

Dalai Lama. *Beyond Dogma: The Challenge of the Modern World*. London: Souvenir Press, 1996.

____________. *An Open Heart: Practising Compassion in Everyday Life*. London: Hodder and Stoughton, 2001.

Dodds, Sarah. "The Former Monk Who Runs a $100m Meditation Firm." *BBC News*. September 2, 2019.
bbc.co.uk

Dvivedi, Kapil Deva. *The Essence of the Vedas*. Bhadohi, Uttar Pradesh: Vishva-Bharati Research Institute, 1990.

Elst, Koenraad. *Who is a Hindu? Hindu Revivalist Views of Animism, Buddhism, Sikhism, and Other Offshoots of Hinduism*. New Delhi: Voice of India, 2002, p. 237.

Fernando, Suman. *Race and Culture in Psychiatry*. London: Croom Helm, 1988.

Fischer, Joel. *Effective Casework Practice: An Eclectic Approach*. New York: McGraw-Hill, 1978.

Flecker, James Elroy. *Hassan: The Story of Hassan of Baghdad and How He Came to Make the Golden Journey to Samarkand*. Palala Press, (1922) 2015. gutenberg.org

Flory, Don. "The Pearl Beyond Price [Interview with A. H. Almaas]." *Yoga Journal*, no. 94 (September/October 1990): 29–32, pp. 29–30.

Freeman, Anthony. "A Daniel Come to Judgement? Dennett and the Revisioning of Transpersonal Theory." *Journal of Consciousness Studies* 13, no. 3 (2006): 95–109.

Frykenberg, Robert Eric. *Christianity in India: From Beginnings to the Present*. Oxford: Oxford University Press, 2008, pp. v, 91.

Gilmour, David. *The British in India: Three Centuries of Ambition and Experience*. London: Allen Lane/Penguin Books, 2018, Chapter 1, Numbers. books.google.co.uk/books

Grant, Pat. "Issues of Cultural Difference in Staff Teams and Client Work." In *Clinical Counselling in Context: An Introduction*, edited by John Lees, 107–120. London: Routledge, 1999, p. 119.

Graves, Robert. *The White Goddess: A Historical Grammar of Poetic Myth*. London: Faber and Faber Ltd, (1948) 2010, p. 380.

Greene, Beverly A. "Considerations in the Treatment of Black Patients by White Therapists." *Psychotherapy* 22(2S) (Summer 1985): 389–393, p. 390.

Grieger, Ingrid, and Joseph G. Ponterotto. "A Framework for Assessment in Multicultural Counseling." In *Handbook of Multicultural Counseling*, edited by Joseph G. Ponterotto, J. Manuel Casas, Lisa A. Suzuki, and Charlene M. Alexander, 357–374. London: Sage Publications, 1995, p. 372.

Guest, Hazel. "The Origins of Transpersonal Psychology." *British Journal of Psychotherapy* 6, no. 1 (1989): 62–69.

Hacking, Ian. *Why Does Language Matter to Philosophy?* Cambridge: Cambridge University Press, 1975, p. 186.

Hall, Edward T. *Beyond Culture*. New York: Anchor Books/Doubleday, (1976) 1989, pp. 30–31.

____________. *The Hidden Dimension*. New York: Anchor Books, (1966) 1990, p. 105.

Harding, Elizabeth U. *Kali: The Black Goddess of Dakshineswar*. Delhi: Motilal Banarsidass, (1993) 1998, p. 54.

Heller, Steven. *The Swastika: Symbol Beyond Redemption?* New York: Allworth Press/Skyhorse Publishing, 2000.

Hesse, Herman. *Steppenwolf*. New York: Herman Holt and Company, 1927.

Hijiya, James A. "The Gita of J. Robert Oppenheimer." In *Proceedings of the American Philosophical Society* 144, no. 2 (2000): 123–167.

Hiriyanna, Mysore. *Essentials of Indian Philosophy*. London: Allen & Unwin, 1949.

Huntingdon, Samuel P. "The Clash of Civilizations?" *Foreign Affairs* 72, no. 3 (Summer 1993): 22–49, p. 22.
dx.doi.org/10.2307/20045621

Internet Sacred Text Archive. *Hinduism: The Vedas*, 2010.
sacred-texts.com/hin/index.htm#vedas

__________. *Emerald Tablet of Hermes*, n.d.
sacred-texts.com/alc/emerald.htm

Jeromson, Barry. "*Systema Munditotius* and *Seven Sermons*: Symbolic Collaborators in Jung's Confrontation with the Dead." *Jung History* 1, no. 2 (Winter 2005–2006): 6–10.

Judith, Anodea. *Eastern Body, Western Mind: Psychology and the Chakra System as a Path to the Self*. Rev. ed. Berkeley: Celestial Arts, (1996) 2004.

Jung, Carl G. *Yoga and the West*. Princeton, NJ: Bollingen Foundation, (1936) 1958, pp. 529–537.

__________. *Psychology and Religion: West and East.* 2nd ed. Translated by R. F. C. Hull. Abingdon, Oxon.: Routledge, (1958) 2014, p. 560.

Kassel, Charles. "Immortality and the New Physics." *North American Review* 216, no. 803 (1922): 523–534.

Kersten, Holger. *Jesus Lived in India*. Shaftesbury, Dorset: Element Books, 1994.

Khan, Talid. "Musings on the Impact of Aniconism and the Practice of Art Therapy Within a Muslim Community." *ATOL: Art Therapy Online* 3, no. 1 (2012).
doi.org/10.25602/GOLD.atol.v3i1.299

Kipling, Rudyard. "The Ballad of East and West" (poem), 1889.
kiplingsociety.co.uk

Koller, John M. *Asian Philosophies*. 6th ed. London: Routledge, (2002) 2017, p. 14.

Korman, Maurice. "National Conference on Levels and Patterns of Professional Training in Psychology: The Major Themes." *American Psychologist* 29, no. 6 (1974): 441–449.

Krishnan, K. S. *Origin of Vedas*. Chennai: Notion Press, 2019.

Lago, Colin. *Race, Culture and Counselling: The Ongoing Challenge.* 2nd ed. Milton Keynes: Open University Press, 2006, p. 68.

Lago, Colin, and Joyce Thompson. *Race, Culture and Counselling.* Milton Keynes: Open University Press, 1996, pp. 55–56.

Lao-tzu. *Tao Te Ching*. Translated by Stephen Mitchell. London: Kyle Cathie Ltd, 2000, p. 7.

Leff, J. P. "Culture and the Differentiation of Emotional States." *British Journal of Psychiatry* 123, no. 574 (1973): 299–306.

Leser, Simon. "The 8 Oldest Religions in the World." *Culture Trip* (April 24, 2018).
theculturetrip.com

Lindtner, Christian. "From Brahmanism to Buddhism." *Asian Philosophy* 9, no. 1 (1999): 5–37.
dx.doi.org/10.1080/09552369908575487

Littlewood, Roland, and Maurice Lipsedge. "Acute Psychotic Reaction in Caribbean-Born Patients." *Psychological Medicine* 11, no. 2 (1981): 303–318.
dx.doi.org/10.1017/S0033291700052120

Loy, David. "Indra's Postmodern Net." *Philosophy East and West* 43, no. 3 (1993): 481–510.
dx.doi.org/10.2307/1399579

McAlpin, David W. "Toward Proto-Elamo-Dravidian." *Language* 50, no. 1 (1974): 89–101.
dx.doi.org/10.2307/412012

———————. "Elamite and Dravidian: Further Evidence of Relationship." *Current Anthropology* 16, no. 1 (1975): 105–115. dx.doi.org/10.1086/201521

Magga, Ole Henrik. "Diversity in Saami Terminology for Reindeer, Snow, and Ice." *International Social Science Journal* 58, no. 187 (2006): 25–34. dx.doi.org/10.1111/j.1468-2451.2006.00594.x

*Maha Upanishad*. Translated by Dr A. G. Krishna Warrier. Wheaton, IL: Theosophical Publishing House, n.d., VI, 72–73[a].

Maltz, Maxwell. *Psycho-Cybernetics*, updated and expanded. New York: Tarcher-Perigee Books/Penguin Random House, (1960) 2015, Preface.

Marsella, Anthony, and Paul Pedersen. *Cross-Cultural Counseling and Psychotherapy*. Pergamon General Psychology Series. London: Pergamon Press, 1981.

Marsella, Anthony, Roland Tharp, and Thomas Ciborowski, eds. *Perspectives on Cross-Cultural Psychology*. New York: Academic Press, 1979.

Menon, Sangeetha. "Hinduism and Science." In *The Oxford Handbook of Religion and Science*, edited by Philip Clayton and Zachary Simpson. Oxford: Oxford University Press, 7–23, 2006, p. 11.

Melchizedek, Drunvalo. *The Ancient Secret of the Flower of Life, Vol. 2*. Flagstaff, AZ: Light Technology Publishing, 1994, p. 65.

Merriam-Webster. 2020. "Alienist." merriam-webster.com

*Metro*. "Zen Behaving Badly . . . ." (May 16, 2019), pp. 18–19.

Moacanin, Radmila. *The Essence of Jung's Psychology and Tibetan Buddhism: Western and Eastern Paths to the Heart*. 2nd ed. Somerville, MA: Wisdom Publications, (1986) 2003, p. 93.

Monier-Williams, Sir Monier. *A Sanskrit-English Dictionary: Etymologically and Philologically Arranged with Special Reference to Cognate Indo-European Languages*. New Delhi: Motilal Banarsidass, (1899) 2011.

Monks of the Ramakrishna Order. *Meditation*. Bourne End, Bucks.: Ramakrishna Vedanta Centre, 1972, p. 53.

Montgomery, Martin. *An Introduction to Language and Society*. Studies in Culture and Communication. 3rd revised ed. Abingdon, Oxon.: Routledge, (1986) 2008.

# REFERENCES

Morgan, Kenneth W., ed. *The Religion of the Hindus*. New Delhi: Motilal Banarsidass, (1953) 1987, p. 79.

Nelson, Libby. "The Charlie Hebdo Attack, Explained." (January 9, 2015). vox.com

Ouspensky, Peter D. *The Fourth Way: A Record of Talks and Answers to Questions Based on the Teachings of G. I. Gurdjieff*. New York: Vintage, (1957) 1971, p. 4.

Oxford University Press. *Oxford Dictionary of English*. 3rd ed. "Ego." Oxford: Oxford University Press, 2010, p. 562.

Paddison, Sarah. *The Hidden Power of the Heart: Discovering an Unlimited Source of Intelligence*. 2nd ed. Boulder Creek, CA: HeartMath (1992) 1998, pp. 217–218, 221, 223.

Padilla, Amado M., and Nelly Salgado de Snyder. "Counseling Hispanics: Strategies for Effective Intervention." In *Handbook of Cross-Cultural Counseling and Therapy*, edited by Paul Pedersen, 157–164. Westport, CT: Greenwood Press, 1985, p. 158.

Pennick, Nigel. *Magical Alphabets*. Newburyport, MA: Red Wheel/Weiser, 1992, pp. 1–2, 12–14, 45.

Philogos. "The Origins of the Precept 'Whoever Saves a Life Saves the World' and What They Tell Us About Particularism and Universalism in Jewish Tradition." *Mosaic Magazine* (October 31, 2016). mosaicmagazine.com

Prabhavananda, Swami, and Christopher Isherwood. *The Yoga Aphorisms of Patanjali*. Chennai: Sri Ramakrishna Math, 1953, pp. 1, 30, 51, 59, 62–68.

Ragaven, Chengiah. "The Philosophy of God Consciousness in the Life of Ramakrishna Paramahamsa," MA thesis in Indian Philosophy. Durban: University of Durban-Westville, Department of Hindu Studies, November 1999, p. 1.

Rolland, Romain. *The Life of Vivekananda and the Universal Gospel*. Almora: Advaita Ashrama, 1953.

Rowan, Arthur. *The Lore of the Bard: A Guide to the Celtic & Druid Mysteries*. London: Llewellyn Publications, 2003, p. 91.

Rowe, Wayne, John T. Behrens, and Mark M. Leach. "Racial Ethnic Identity and Racial Consciousness: Looking Back and Looking Forward." In *Handbook of Multicultural Counseling*, edited by Joseph G. Ponterotto, J. Manuel Casas, Lisa A. Suzuki, and Charlene M. Alexander, 218–235. London: Sage Publications, 1995.

Ryan, Joseph F. "Photography as a Tool of Awareness." *Journal of Transpersonal Psychology* 44, no. 1 (2012): 92–97, p. 95.

Śaṅkarācārya, Sri. *Self-Knowledge: An English Translation of Śaṅkarāchārya's Ātmabodha with Notes, Comments, and Introduction by Swāmi Nikhilānanda.* Chennai: Sri Ramakrishna Math, 1947.

Sapir, Edward. "Conceptual Categories in Primitive Languages." *Science* 74 (1931): 578. [Abstract of paper presented to the autumn meeting of the National Academy of Sciences, New Haven, CT, November 16–18, 1931.]

Satprakashananda, Swami. *Hinduism and Christianity: Jesus Christ and His Teachings in the Light of Vedanta.* St. Louis, MO: Vedanta Society of St Louis, 1975.

Scharfstein, Ben-Ami. *Philosophy East/Philosophy West: A Critical Comparison of Indian, Chinese, Islamic, and European Philosophy.* Oxford: Basil Blackwell, 1978, pp. 9, 15, 18, 120, 140.

Schlosser, Marco, Terje Sparby, Sebastjan Vörös, Rebecca Jones, and Natalie L. Marchant. "Unpleasant Meditation-Related Experiences in Regular Meditators: Prevalence, Predictors, and Conceptual Considerations." *PLoS ONE* 14, no. 5 (2019): e0216643.
dx.doi.org/10.1371/journal.pone.0216643

Schmidt, Bettina E., and Lucy Huskinson, eds. *Spirit Possession and Trance: New Interdisciplinary Perspectives.* London and New York: Continuum, 2010.

Shakespear, John. *A Dictionary, Hindūstānī and English, with a Copious Index, Fitting the Work to Serve, also, as a Dictionary English and Hindūstānī.* J. L. Cox and Son, printers. Sold by Allen, Parbury, & Co., (1817) 1834, p. 176.
books.google.hu/books

Sharma, Meera. "The Bridge: Linking the Gap Between Eastern and Western Psychology, Spirituality, Language and Culture." MA thesis in Psychotherapy and Counselling. London: Regent's School, School of Psychotherapy and Counselling, September 2002.

__________. "Trans-personal & Psychology of the Vedic System: Healing the Split Between Psychology and Spirituality." *International Journal of Yoga and Allied Sciences* 4, no. 1 (January–June 2015a): 41–48, p. 41.

_________. "Meditation and Yoga in the West." *International Journal of Science and Consciousness* [Review article] 1, no. 2 (December 2015b): 1–8, p. 3.

_________. "The Subjective View of Life 'Evenness of Mind Is Yoga. Equanimity Within Is Spiritual Life' (Gita: 2-48)" [Conceptual paper]. *MOJ Yoga & Physical Therapy* 2, no. 3 (2017a): 68–72, p. 71.

_________. "The Therapeutic Application of Yoga." Paper presented at the International Conference on Social Transformation Through Yoga, Haridwar, India, March 2017b, p. 3.

Sharma, Meera, and Joseph F. Ryan. "Bridging West and East Through the Transpersonal Approach of Psychotherapy." *International Journal of Yoga and Allied Sciences* 3, no. 1 (January–June 2014): 68–75, p. 69.

_________________________. "The Relationship Between Yoga Psychology and Western Psychology and Its Implications for Psychotherapy." *International Journal of Yoga and Allied Sciences* 6, no. 1 (January–June 2017): 50–61, p. 50.

_________________________. "A Journey of Awakening: The Emergence of Consciousness." *MOJ Yoga & Physical Therapy* 3, no. 5 (2018): 110–114, p. 113. doi: 10.15406/mojypt.2018.03.00056

Shearer, A., and P. Russell (trans.). *The Upanishads*. New York: Harper and Row, 1978, p. 8.

Sheldrake, Philip. *Spirituality: A Brief History*. 2nd ed. Oxford: Wiley-Blackwell, (2007) 2013.

Shonin, Edo, William Van Gordon, and Mark D. Griffiths. "The Emerging Role of Buddhism in Clinical Psychology: Toward Effective Integration." *Psychology of Religion and Spirituality* 6, no. 2 (2014): 123–137.

Shweder, Richard A. "Menstrual Pollution, Soul Loss, and the Comparative Study of Emotions." In *Culture and Depression: Studies in the Anthropology and Cross-Cultural Psychiatry of Affect and Disorder*, edited by Arthur Kleinman, and Byron Good, 182–215. Berkeley, CA: University of California Press, 1985, pp. 193–200.

Singer, June K. *Boundaries of the Soul: The Practice of Jung's Psychology*. Rev. ed. Anchor, 1994.

Singh, Balmiki Prasad. *India's Culture: The State, the Arts and Beyond*. Oxford: Oxford University Press, 1998, pp. 147, 196.

_________. "Understanding India." *Dialogue* 8, no. 1 (July–September 2006).

Singh, Jaideva. *Śiva Sūtras: The Yoga of Supreme Identity*. Channai: Motilal Banarsidass, 1979, pp. 117–118, 126.

Sivananda, Swami. *Essence of the Chandogya Upanishad*. Sivanandaonline.org. The Divine Life Society, 2011, para. 61.
sivanandaonline.org

Smith, Edward E., and Douglas L. Medin. *Concepts and Categories*. Cambridge, MA: Harvard University Press, 1981, p. 1.

Sparavigna, Amelia Carolina. "The Creation of the World in the Sefer Yetzirah," *International Journal of Sciences* 3, no. 5 (May 2014): 11-17.

Stone, John R., ed. *The Essential Max Müller: On Language, Mythology, and Religion*. New York: Palgrave Macmillan, 2002, p. 59.

Sue, Derald Wing, Patricia Arrendondo, and Roderick J. McDavis. "Multicultural Counseling Competencies and Standards: A Call to the Profession." In *Handbook of Multicultural Counseling*, edited by Joseph G. Ponterotto, J. Manuel Casas, Lisa A. Suzuki, and Charlene M. Alexander, 624–640. London: Sage Publications, 1995.

Sue, Derald Wing, and David Sue. *Counselling the Culturally Different: Theory and Practice*. London: Wiley, 1990, p. 137.

Suresh, Padmaja. "Abhinavagupta's Definition of Moksha." *Hindu* (August 1, 2019).
thehindu.com

Temperton, James. "'Now I Am Become Death, the Destroyer of Worlds.' The Story of Oppenheimer's Infamous Quote." *Wired* (August 9, 2017).
wired.co.uk

Teresa, Mother. *A Simple Path*. Compiled by Lucinda Vardey. London: Rider Books/Penguin Ebury, 1995.

Thompson. Geoff. *The Divine CEO: Creating a Divine Covenant*. UK: O-Books/John Hunt Publishing, 2020, p. 9.

Tigunait, Pandit R. *Seven Systems of Indian Philosophy*. Honesdale, PA: Himalayan International Institute of Yoga Science and Philosophy of the U.S.A., 1983, pp. 7, 21, 144, 155.

Toffler, Alvin. *Future Shock*. New York: Random House, (1970) 1990.

Urban Dictionary (n.d.). "Bad."
urbandictionary.com

Vasudaikakutumbam. "Vasudhaiva Kutumbakam." (March 5, 2015).
vasudaikakutumbam.wordpress.com

Vedanta Society of New York. "Vedanta Society of New York History." (2018).
vedantany.org

Vedic Foundation. "Definition of Bharatvarsh." (2006).
thevedicfoundation.org

Venkatesh, Karthik. "Prakrit: The Forgotten Ancestor." *Mint* (September 2, 2018).
livemint.com

Vivekananda, Swami. *From Colombo to Almora: Being a Record of the Swami Vivekananda's Return to India after his Mission to the West, Including Reports of Seventeen Lectures.* Chennai [formerly Madras]: Vyjayanti Press, 1897.

__________________. *Jnana Yoga.* Mayawati, Uttarakhan: Advaita Ashrama, 1955.

__________________. *Religion of Love.* Baghbazar: Udbodhan, 1960, pp. 59–62.

__________________. *Pearls of Wisdom.* Kolkata: Ramakrishna Mission Institute of Culture, (1998) 2010.

__________________. *Complete Works.* Hollywood, CA: Vedanta Press & Catalog, 2018, pp. 734, 738.

Vontress, Clemmont E. "Racial and Ethnic Barriers in Counselling." In *Counseling Across Cultures*, edited by Paul B. Pedersen, Juris G. Draguns, Walter J. Lonner, and Joseph E. Trimble, 87–107. Honolulu: University of Hawaii Press, 1981.

Vygotsky, L. S. [Lev Semyonovich]. "The Genesis of Higher Mental Functions." In *Cognitive Development to Adolescence*, edited by K. Richardson, and S. Sheldon, 61–80. Mahwah, NJ: Erlbaum, 1988, p. 74.

Wallwork, J. F. *Language and Linguistics: An Introduction to the Study of Language.* New York: Heinemann Educational Books, 1969, p. 154.

Walsh, Roger, and Frances Vaughan, eds. *Paths Beyond Ego: The Transpersonal Vision.* New York: Jeremy P. Tarcher/Putnam, 1993, p. 154.

Wang, William. S.-Y., ed. *The Emergence of Language Development and Evolution.* Berkeley, CA: University of California Press, 1991.

Warner, Brad. *Letters to a Dead Friend about Zen.* Novato, CA: New World Library, 2019. Chapters 2, 5, 6, 9, 15, 17, 21, 24.

Washington, Gill. "Song of Mahamudra by Tilopa." From *Teachings of the Buddha*, edited by Jack Kornfield (June 17, 2014). allspirit.co.uk

Welwood, John, ed. *Awakening the Heart.* Berkeley, CA: Shambhala, 1985, p. 41.

Wikipedia. "Ātman (Hinduism)." (September 27, 2020).

_________. "Languages with Official Status in India." (September 12, 2019).

_________. "List of Endangered Languages in India." (April 12, 2019).

_________. "Mindfulness." (December 1, 2019).

_________. "Vyasa." (February 1, 2020).

Wilber, Ken. *No Boundary: Eastern and Western Approaches to Personal Growth.* Berkeley, CA: Shambhala, 1985.

_________. *Grace and Grit: Spirituality and Healing in the Life of Treya Killam Wilber.* Berkeley, CA: Shambhala, 1991.

_________. *The Spectrum of Consciousness.* Wheaton, IL: Theosophical Publishing House, (1977) 1993.

_________. *The Eye of Spirit: An Integral Vision for a World Gone Slightly Mad.* 3rd ed. Boston and London: Shambhala, (1997) 2001, p. 231.

_________. *One Taste: Daily Reflections on Integral Spirituality.* Rev. ed. Berkeley, CA: Shambhala, 2000, pp. 19, 30.

Zajonc, Arthur, ed. *The New Physics and Cosmology: Dialogues with the Dalai Lama.* Oxford: Oxford University Press, 2004, pp. 103–104.

Zamonski, Kathy, Linda A. Marshall, Dodi Matheny Wozniak, Marty Davis Cottrill, and Karen Ander Francis. *Sophia's Table: Women's Wisdom in Five Voices.* Bloomington, IN: AuthorHouse, 2013, p. 39.

Zukav, Gary. *The Dancing Wu Li Masters: An Overview of the New Physics.* New York: Bantam Books, (1979) 2001.

# Acknowledgements

## *Meera Sharma*

I would like to acknowledge my gratitude to Dr. Joseph F. Ryan, co-author of this book, my student, supervisee, and a very good friend, indeed. It is due to his efforts, dedication, and appreciation of my work that made it possible for this book to be published. He not only inspired me but also devoted much time and energy to the final editing of the manuscript. I also wish to acknowledge my gratitude to Dr. Kamakhya Kumar from Uttarakhand Sanskrit University, Haridwar, India, for his encouragement and support. Grateful thanks are also due to both my sons—Vivek Sharma and Padma Aon Prakasha—for inspiring me and providing insights through meaningful discussions. I also wish to acknowledge a number of scholars and practitioners who have contributed through stimulating discussions to the final form of this book. Finally, Joseph and I would like to thank TransPersonal Press publisher Thierry Bogliolo for his belief in our book and support during the publishing process, and editor Nicky Leach for the depth of her understanding of our material, engagement with the book, and editorial input.

## *Joseph Ryan*

Many thanks to Meera Sharma, who has been my counselling tutor, clinical supervisor, co-author, and friend; my wife, Edina Bozsó-Ryan, for her love, patience, and understanding; the Bozsó family—István ("Pisti"), Kriszti, Péter ("Peti"), Petra, and Levente ("Levi")—in Felsözsolca, Hungary, for their hospitality while I worked on the manuscript; Hannah McWilliams for telling me about Caleb Carr's novel, *The Alienist*, then pointing out a copy to me in a bookshop; Rui N., whose encouragement and support helped to make it possible; Talid Khan for alerting me to his paper; and my colleagues, supervisees, and clients, who all contribute to the development of my understanding.

# About the Authors

## *Meera Sharma,* MA

Meera Sharma is a transpersonal psychotherapist, supervisor, and trainer, and has worked at a number of academic institutions and agencies. Her Trinity Model builds a bridge between Eastern and Western psychological approaches. Meera is the founder of the Centre for Spiritual and Transpersonal Studies (CSTS), London, England, which offers a variety of courses and workshops. She can be contacted at: msharma669@aol.com

## *Joseph F. Ryan,* PhD

Dr. Joseph Ryan graduated with Highest Honours in History and Political Science from Carleton University, Ottawa, Canada. He also has a PhD in History from the University of Hull, England; and an MSc in Psychology and an MA in Creative Writing from Kingston University, London. Early in his career, Joseph practised for many years as a Registered Nurse, served with the Royal Army Medical Corps (Reserve) as a medic, and was later employed at the Ministry of Defence. Dr. Ryan is now a transpersonal counsellor and clinical supervisor, working mainly in the field of addiction and, in particular, with those affected by the addictions of their loved ones. Joseph worked at the Priory Hospital, Roehampton, on the Addiction Treatment Programme (ATP) for many years, as well as at the Addiction Support and Care Agency (ASCA), Kingston and Richmond. Joseph is the author or editor of many books and articles. He practises Zen meditation with the Jogye Order of Korean Buddhism and lives peacefully next to the River Thames, close to Hampton Court Palace, Surrey. Dr. Ryan may be contacted at: joseph_ryan@btinternet.com

# Also available

To celebrate its 30 years of pioneering work in the fields of counselling and psychotherapy training, the Re-Vision Centre for Transpersonal & Integrative Therapy has brought together a selection of writing by practitioners and teachers who have worked at the heart of the organization.

The chapters address a social and cultural crisis which, at this point in the history of our planet, needs new ways of looking at therapy and how it relates to the world beyond the consulting room. Just as 'the personal is political' was a way of seeing individual issues within the context of a wider political field, so we now need to see that the soul is a different kind of agency from that of the ego – one that is both internal and external, individual and cultural. The world may have lost connection with soul in its obsession with merchandise and control, but soul has not lost connection with us. These chapters offer an integrative perspective that both gives a place to the troubles of the modern world and also develops a well-tuned craft to firstly attend to our painful wounds and ultimately transform their bitterness into the salt of wisdom.

This book is a compelling work for psychotherapists, counsellors, trainees, and anyone interested in how psychotherapy influences and is influenced by the state of the planet, by imagination and by the reality of how politics impact on our daily lives.

ISBN 978-1-912-618-02-8 (print) / 978-1-912618-03-5 (ebook)

TransPersonal
Press

# Also available

*Transpersonal Dynamics* offers approaches to the therapeutic encounter from the leading edge of quantum physics field theory and integrative psychology.

*Transpersonal Dynamics* is the culmination of over 20 years of feedback about 'what works', gathered through delivering integrative and transpersonal training to counsellors, coaches, psychologists and psychotherapists who work with organisations, adults, couples, families, young people and children.

Using down-to-earth language in a practical way, this book addresses some of the gritty aspects of the therapeutic relationship, with the aim to inspire and support practitioners to take more risks to bring a collaborative, relational quality to their work.

*Stacey Millichamp is a trainer on the Masters Degree in Psychotherapy and the Diploma in Integrative and Transpersonal Clinical Supervision at the* Psychosynthesis Trust *in London, and teaches on the Diploma in Supervision with Soul at the* Re-Vision Centre for Integrative Psychosynthesis *in London. She is the Director of* Entrust Associates, *which provides counselling to staff and students of secondary and primary schools in London.*

isbn 978-1-912-618-00-4 (print) / 978-1-912618-00-1 (ebook)

TransPersonal
Press